Message Me

The Future of Customer Service in the Era
of Social Messaging and Artificial Intelligence

Joshua March
CEO, Conversocial

ISBN: 978-1-54393-371-0 (print)

ISBN: 978-1-54391-354-5 (ebook)

TABLE OF CONTENTS

ACKNOWLEDGEMENTS

When I set out to write *Message Me*, my inherent bias to over-optimism meant I was certain it could be written in just a few months. Almost a year later, after many interviews, revisions, and re-writes, I've realized that writing a book—even a relatively concise one such as this—is a big labor of love that demands not just a huge amount of focused individual dedication, but also a lot of time and effort from all the many people involved in the process. I owe considerable debt for the generous feedback I received on various chapters (and my writing style) that have made this into a much better book than my first draft ever could have been.

I want to give special thanks to the Conversocial customers and my industry peers who gave their time for extensive interviews and case studies, including: Chris Moody (formerly GM Data Products at Twitter), who has been a great partner and mentor to me; Frankie Saucier (formerly Senior Manager, Social Media and Support Chat at Cox Communications), whose understanding of the complex analytical needs of a highly scaled customer service environment had a major impact on how I think about the measurement of customer care over social messaging; Alison Herzog (Director of Global Social Business at Dell), who has rare insight into the operations of one of the largest social care operations in the world; Adam Devine (SVP and Head of Marketing at WorkFusion), who gave valuable input into how artificial intelligence is being used in back-office tasks; Shane Mac (cofounder of Assist), who over many conversations has helped shape my thinking of the potential for bots and automation in messaging, and who is building one of the most exciting companies in this space; and Dan Moriarty (Digital Director, Chicago Bulls and previously Director, Digital

Strategy and Activation at Hyatt Hotels), who was an amazing innovation partner at Hyatt, working with us to help drive the industry forward.

I also want to thank everyone at Conversocial (past and present) who has been with me on this incredible journey so far. The thinking in this book has been directly impacted by every single one of you over thousands of conversations and the amazing work you've put into helping our customers over the years. I especially want to call out Mathew Munro, Ido Bornstein-HaCohen, Christy O'Reilly and Chris Venus who gave heavy input and feedback into some of the chapters and ideas you'll read in the book. Thank you to Chris Pemberton for editorial, research and writing support.

And finally, a special thank you to Dr. Jon Krohn, Chief Data Scientist at untapt and presenter of Deep Learning with TensorFlow (LiveLessons in O'Reilly Safari), and Neri Van Otten, Senior Data Scientist Consultant, for the valuable feedback on the chapters covering artificial intelligence (AI) and many conversations on the development of Deep Learning and the practical application of AI techniques into messaging.

PREFACE

When I founded Conversocial at the beginning of 2010, we were building general social media software, designed to help the social media teams of big brands manage the growing presences they were developing on sites like Facebook and Twitter. But over the course of that year, I came to a major realization: these platforms weren't just the latest marketing gimmick. They were profoundly changing how people communicated with friends, family, and with brands. I realized that as all communications continued to shift into smartphones, social media, and mobile messaging, these channels would fundamentally change how companies communicated and delivered service to their customers. I knew that social media couldn't remain as an island in the social media or marketing teams—it would need to be deeply integrated into every business unit, including customer service.

At the beginning of 2011, we started working with Tesco, a major, multi-billion-dollar retailer in the UK. They shared our vision, and asked us to help them integrate social media into their customer service team. I started traveling to their major contact centers around the UK, watching as customer service teams attempted to deliver service over social media, but with tools that had been designed for marketing. I sat with agents as they struggled to piece together the background to a customer's complaint across several messages. I saw supervisors spend days painstakingly creating manual reports on productivity and performance—without the right data. But at the end, I also witnessed thousands of customers who had turned to these channels for help—and were ecstatic that their issues were getting resolved, quickly and easily, in the same channel that they used to reach out.

This engagement crystallized what became the singular mission of Conversocial: to bridge the gap between the rapidly shifting world of social and mobile channels with the needs of large enterprise contact centers. We had a vision for how the world of customer service was changing, and our mission was to help companies take their contact centers into this new world.

Since then, we have built the leading solution to help companies deliver large-scale, enterprise-grade customer service over social media and mobile messaging channels. We were the first platform to launch full live-chat capabilities on Facebook Messenger, the first Instagram Community Management Partner, and we recently launched a new, exclusive partnership with Twitter where we are working together on unique customer service functionality for our clients. Today, hundreds of the world's biggest brands—from Google to Hyatt Hotels and Alaska Airlines—partner with Conversocial to deliver customer service over social media and mobile messaging.

There's no doubt the growth of social media has had a tremendous impact on the customer service world. But now the world of customer service is about to change again—this time with an even bigger impact.

Over the past couple of years, we've observed incredible growth in social messaging applications, the launch of bot platforms that allow deeper interactive experiences (and even payments) within messaging conversations and massive developments in artificial intelligence (AI). The convergence of these trends will radically transform customer service over the next five years. Are you, and your organization, ready?

Today, I can run my business almost entirely using apps on my phone, and I can order anything I can dream of at the touch of a button. Yet when it comes to getting help, too often companies still make me call, wait on hold, and jump through hoops. I've intuitively felt all along—as an employee, CEO, and consumer—that effortless, convenient, and seamless experiences are key to keep customers coming back and recommending your brand to their friends. That's why making customer service easy for both consumers and brands is what Conversocial is all about.

This isn't just me. In the customer service world, there has been a growing understanding that the general approach to service that many companies take is not working. With huge numbers of customers still phoning the call center (to great expense) companies have worked tirelessly to make it harder and harder to actually speak to a human. But with most digital channels still failing to fully deliver, most customers still end up phoning—after jumping through many frustrating hoops along the way. A new mindset is required.

The best summary of this thinking is *Effortless Experience* by Matt Dixon, Nick Toman, and Rick DeLisi from the Corporate Executive Board (now part of Gartner). Reading this, I was struck by the book's central insight that when it comes to increasing customer loyalty through customer service, a focus on lowering effort when there's a problem or issue—not delivering over-the-top delight—is what moves the needle. This insight flew in the face of decades of conventional wisdom that delight at all costs is what mattered. I highly recommend this book to anyone in the service world, and regularly send copies out to clients and partners. However, although the research in the book is fundamental to my view of the correct approach to customer service, I believe the tools to actually deliver on the promise of an "effortless experience" are only now becoming widely available.

A massive driver of this is the growth of messaging. Messaging has become the default paradigm for all communication—social messaging apps among friends, Slack messaging among colleagues, and LinkedIn messaging among business contacts. While WeChat has become the default place for businesses to transact and serve consumers in China, Facebook Messenger and Twitter have been adding functionality at a rapid clip to enable real-time chat, automation, and interactive experiences, making it easier for brands to create effortless experiences that get consumers the right answer, at the right time, whatever channel they are on.

But in the years since *Effortless Experience* was published, despite all these new developments, it seems it's gotten harder, not easier, for service leaders to deliver seamless, convenient care.

More channels and more choices mean more confusion. Despite the incredible product advances by Facebook Messenger, Twitter, and the other social media platforms and third-party solution providers, it's getting harder for brands to leave their legacy mindset behind and adopt a forward-looking vision for easy 21st century customer service. There's a gap between knowing you need to chart a new course to seamless service experiences and actually taking the concrete steps needed to start the journey. This challenge is only exacerbated by rapid advances in AI, machine learning, social messaging, and big data. There seems to be more questions than answers. Where to start? What to stop? What investments will make demonstrable improvements in ease of use and customer effort? How do I make sense of the forces changing customer expectations right in front of my eyes?

It's going to take a whole lot more than just a single platform or service to deliver the kind of "just-hit-the-easy-button" service that consumers expect in an age of social messaging and AI. Service leaders will have to understand the forces shaping the modern service experience from the customer perspective and from the company perspective. They'll have to be able to see around the corner to spot oncoming technologies poised to fundamentally alter the playing field. And they'll need to take specific actions along key strategic fronts if they are to be positioned for success in this new era.

Part roadmap, part storybook and part toolbox, Part 1 of this book outlines the major forces that are shaping customer service today and tomorrow, then Part 2 sets out a clear outline of the steps service leaders and executives need to take in order to be ready for a future of care dominated by social media, messaging and AI.

My family is completely spread out across the globe. I'm English but live in New York City. My mother lives in Kenya. My father lives in Scotland. One brother lives in Australia, another in Germany, and I have uncles and cousins across the United Kingdom and the United States. The only easy way to stay in touch is through messaging apps. We have various WhatsApp groups for different parts of the family and are always messaging, sending voice memos, photos and videos to each other. It's how a modern family stays together. And all day, I'm interacting with my industry and getting news from Twitter, and I'm on Slack with my colleagues. I live in an asynchronous, messaging, mobile world. If I need to get an answer from a brand to fix an issue, it's incredibly easy for me to start a chat with them in Messenger or send them a Twitter DM—but only if they are there.

I tell my family and friends to message me.

Why can't a brand just "message me"?

PART ONE

The Forces Shaping Modern Customer Service

CHAPTER 1

We Live in an Effortless World... Almost

* *

I've never met anyone who likes calling a business.

—Mark Zuckerberg, Facebook CEO, at the 2016 F8 Developer conference[1]

When I landed in New York recently, where I've lived for the last five years, a notification popped up automatically from my Delta app telling me the carousel where my bag would arrive. After picking up my bag, I ordered a Lyft that arrived in minutes to whisk me home. During the journey, I opened Postmates and ordered dinner, which arrived just minutes after I walked into my apartment. And while eating dinner, I opened up the Salesforce app to check on the progress of new sales deals while I'd been traveling.

It's now possible to do almost anything through a smartphone app. You can run your business, you can control the lights in your home, you can order almost anything to your door in minutes, and you can even—with Tinder—find true love (or whatever kind of love you're looking for).

The world is forging ahead. But customer service hasn't caught up yet.

According to dialahuman.com, to speak to a live customer service representative to resolve an issue with one brand's 401(k) plan, you'll need to call their 800 number, press 1, then press the pound button (#) 17 times. Not once, not twice, but 17 times to get an actual human.

Not exactly effortless.

Unfortunately, for too many companies this is the norm and not the exception. Reaching an actual human being to resolve an issue is now so cumbersome and difficult, an entire service ecosystem has emerged to assist consumers in navigating the maze of phone tree prompts. Dialahuman.com is a self-service directory of phone tree hacks. GetHuman.com is another "it's-crazy-we-need-this" website squarely aimed at taking the sting out of navigating customer service phone trees. In an era where consumers have powerful handheld smartphones that get reception nearly anywhere in the world, it should be easier than this to get the solution you need, when you need it, with as much effort as it takes to send a text message.

There's a disconnect between the mental models of today's service teams and the evolving service expectations of consumers.

There's a disconnect between the mental models of today's service teams and the evolving service expectations of consumers. Service teams gaze into the rearview mirror, giving lip-service to delighting customers while often just making it as hard as possible to actually get an issue resolved—while consumers have ever increasing expectations of instant answers, whenever they want it, delivered in the same way they now interact with their friends and the world around them: through beautifully designed, simple to use mobile apps and effortless mobile messaging.

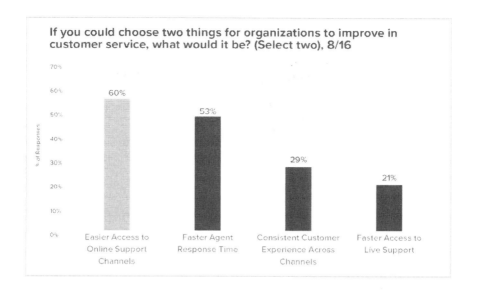

If you could choose two things for organizations to improve in customer service, what would it be? (Select two), 8/16

% of Responses

| | 60% | 53% | 29% | 21% |

- Easier Access to Online Support Channels
- Faster Agent Response Time
- Consistent Customer Experience Across Channels
- Faster Access to Live Support

In a survey in 2016, the analyst firm Ovum found that "easier access to online support channels" was the biggest request from consumers, of all ages. Consumer preference is clear, but companies still have to catch up.[2]

THE PROBLEM WITH TODAY'S SERVICE MODEL

The *Effortless Experience* authors asked a key question at the heart of modern competition: "Should companies try to create differentiation and build customer loyalty by delivering superior service?" It's a crucial question in an age of product and service commoditization and razor thin margins. Given the cutthroat and expensive competition to acquire and keep a customer, the authors wanted to know to what extent customer service impacted loyalty, and what service leaders should be focusing on in order to make the most impact.

They discovered powerful insights that profoundly impact the future of customer service, and underpin how brands can leverage social messaging and AI to deliver easy service:

A strategy of delight doesn't pay

The authors' analysis and data showed that customers who are moved from a level of "below expectations" up to "meets expectations" offer about the *same* economic value as those whose experiences were exceeded[3]. From a customer's perspective, when something goes wrong, the overriding sentiment is: *just help me fix it.*

Many companies today are stuck between the pressure to decrease service costs (usually by making it hard to reach an agent) and the pressure to maintain customer loyalty (by attempting to make the service experience, when you finally get to it, as "delightful" as possible). But they're focusing on the wrong things.

Customer service interactions tend to drive disloyalty, not loyalty

Customers go to a brand because of product features—but they tend to leave a brand because of poor service experiences. Unfortunately, the authors noted that "*any* customer service interaction is *four times* more likely to drive *disloyalty* than to drive loyalty."[4]

According to Dixon, Toman and DeLisi, key drivers that impact disloyalty include (in order of impact): more than one contact to resolve, generic service, repeating information, additional effort to resolve, and transfers between agents or channels. Sound familiar? Making a customer jump through hoops and repeat themselves to finally get through to an agent creates a hugely negative experience, no matter how great that final agent ends up being.

The end result is that it's now easier to order a competitor's product on Amazon Prime than get a solution for the broken widget in our hand. What should companies do instead?

EASY IS EVERYTHING

In order for service organizations to catch up, executives need to put "customer effort" at the core of their experience design. This is the key measure to ensure that service interactions are not driving disloyalty. As Dixon, Toman and DeLisi noted in *Effortless Experience:* "Companies should focus on making service easier, not more delightful, by reducing the amount of work required of customers to get their issues resolved. This includes avoiding their having to repeat information, having to repeatedly contact the company, switching channels, being transferred and being treated in a generic manner."[5] In our own consumer research, more than two-thirds (67.8%) of respondents agree that the easier a customer service interaction is, the more likely he or she would be to engage that brand again.[6]

These findings provide clear and compelling guidance for service leaders. Consumers expect service to be easy: and easy is defined as fast, convenient, and delivered in the original channel (don't ask me to phone or email when I message or tweet you!).

THE END OF WAITING ON HOLD

Customers don't want to use the phone. In *Effortless Experience*, the authors found that, on average, 58% of a company's call volume is from customers who tried to resolve their issue digitally first. Almost two-thirds of all phone calls could have been deflected with better digital care.

At the same time, companies in America spend tens of billions of dollars on answering customer service phone calls every single year, and are under constant pressure to do whatever they can to reduce this number. But despite everyone's best efforts, the mainstream digital channels available today have only made a minor impact on the number of calls made every year. It takes days to get an email response from most companies, so consumers will never use it for anything urgent. Chat is great if you're sitting at your desktop computer, but requires constant attention—and if you lose your session you have to start all over again. And traditional self-service forums require a lot of manual searching—i.e., effort—to discover answers. So customers pick up the phone instead, and the cycle continues.

Messaging is the first channel to emerge that can change this, by combining the in-the-moment speed of chat with the asynchronous convenience of email.

DELIVERING IN-CHANNEL RESOLUTION WHEREVER THE CUSTOMER IS

The traditional approach to service has been to funnel requests into the channels that are easiest and cheapest for companies to deliver—regardless of how easy or convenient they are for consumers. If you're a monopoly provider then you may still be able to get away with offering limited phone support only, 9–5. But for everyone else, convenience is key—and this means delivering service wherever your customers are, whenever they need it.

Once customers started tweeting complaints, the standard response from most companies was to ask them to contact customer service by emailing or phoning. The thoughts and tweets from consumers in return were … "What? This *is* me contacting you!" Deflection to other channels is the worst possible response to give to someone who has reached out—especially if they're reaching out *because* they've already had a bad service experience on other channels. And this isn't even limited to social media—many companies offer differing levels of service on different channels, forcing customers to channel switch to get their issue resolved—an immensely frustrating experience and a major cause of disloyalty. Focusing on 'first contact resolution' is irrelevant if you only offer this over the phone (and only after going through a painful phone tree to get to an agent). Deflecting customers from one channel to another is not only damaging to the customer relationship, but also means your agents must respond to the same issue on multiple channels, increasing complexity and expense. Enabling consumers to quickly and effortlessly get resolution in their original channel is critical, whatever channel that is. With the ability today to securely authenticate customers over social and messaging channels, there is no excuse to not deliver full resolution wherever your customers are. It is simply a matter of will (and sometimes executive support).

THE RISE OF IN-THE-MOMENT EXPECTATIONS

I'm sure I'm not alone in getting angry with my phone when I call an Uber only to find I have to wait more than 5 minutes for a car to arrive. I had to wait 20 minutes on hold to speak to my bank recently (after their social team deflected my tweet), and I was so upset about my time being wasted that I was almost kicking the curb. The CEB authors found that "a whopping 84% of customers simply want their issue resolved as quickly and easily as possible ...."[7] We live in a hyper convenient, hyper mobile, and hyper social world. Customer service needs to keep up.

> Spending 15 minutes wading through a web self-help page only to call an agent and be put on hold for 45 minutes doesn't cut it anymore.

Over the last five years, I've watched as customer expectations of response times in social media have crept down. First, an hour. Then 30 minutes. Then 15. Now, the best brands respond in just minutes. If you tweet at Alaska Airlines, you'll get an answer to your question in under 3 minutes, on average. If you want these channels to deflect phone calls, this is the speed of response you need—and customers need to know they'll get it. Spending 15 minutes wading through a web self-help page only to call an agent and be put on hold for 45 minutes (while your tweets are being ignored) doesn't cut it anymore.

CASE STUDY: MAKING CUSTOMER SERVICE "EASY" AT BRITISH TELECOM

In the highly competitive world of telecoms, customer service is a key differentiator. Good customer service reduces churn, drives loyalty, and can increase customer value through the sale of additional products and services. British Telecom (BT) had a goal of creating the best customer service in the market, and identified that the "ease" of customer service was a major factor in reducing churn and impacting customer loyalty and advocacy. They decided to focus on tracking customer effort instead of the more standard Net Promoter Score. Applying this insight, BT created a "Net Easy" score using the question "How easy was it to get the help you wanted from BT today?" with the potential answers a simple "Easy," "Neither/Don't know," or "Difficult." The Net Easy score was the percentage of respondents who answered "Easy" minus the percentage of respondents who answered "Difficult."

They gave this survey to customers who contacted them across different service channels in order to measure not only the impact of effort on customer churn but also to assess what the best channel strategy should be.

The results were definitive: *customers who had an "easy" service interaction were 40% less likely to churn than customers who had a "difficult" service interaction.*

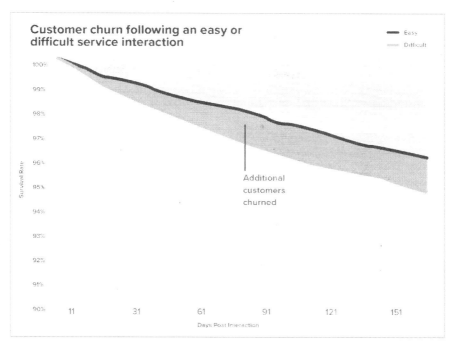

Churn rates were lower among customers who had an "easy" experience of dealing with BT. The chart above shows the percentage of customers with different experiences of the group who stayed with it as time passed from their interaction.[8]

BT also found that social media outscored other channels, including email, online self-service and voice. According to their "Net Easy" scores, social media outperformed phone by 4:1, and outperformed email and self-service by 2:1. As a result, BT began to promote social care as a channel, successfully routing 600,000 contacts a year to social media, saving an estimated £2m a year.[9]

KEY TAKEAWAYS

- To have the biggest impact on loyalty, customer service organizations should focus on reducing customer effort—not on delighting customers.

- Customers go to digital channels first, but because today those channels either aren't fast enough or aren't convenient enough, a majority of people end up phoning the call center.

- To switch to a model of effortless service you need to make it easy for your customers to connect with you, which means being available in the channels they already use, and committing to delivering consistent, full resolution in these channels.

- Customers expect a rapid response, in their moment of need—taking hours to respond digitally is a guaranteed way to ensure they phone you as well.

- Reducing the effort of service interactions has been shown to improve customer retention—and social media and mobile messaging have been found to be lower effort for service than phone, email, and self-service.

CHAPTER 2

Customers Have Changed Forever

• •

In the light of the evolution of the supercharged,
superconnected so-called "autonomous customer," power is
often shifting from corporate to customer as they tap into the
power of the social and smart technologies available to them.

—Dr. Nicola J. Millard, Customer Experience Futurologist,
BT Global Services[10]

Hasan Syed was angry. Really angry. The airline he flew had lost his father's bags, and after two days trying to get the airline to answer his emails, he attempted to message them on Twitter as well. But after multiple attempts at basic communication that were all ignored without acknowledgement, he became increasingly irate. Mr. Syed decided to up the ante. He spent $1,000 of his own money to promote an angry tweet to over 50,000 complete strangers. From this the tweet went viral, blowing up into a major PR crisis. Mr. Syed "went nuclear" not so much because of the lost bags, but because of the lack of a fast reply or acknowledgement of his problem (on Twitter or any other channel), neither in the moment of need nor two days after the fact. After the PR blow up, the airline acknowledged his issue and pledged to look into it—but the damage was already done.

Contrast Mr. Syed's experience with that of a Great Western Railways (GWR) customer I'll call Sarah. After a mishap on a commute home,

Sarah sent an upset message to GWR over Facebook Messenger. A GWR social care agent responded in just 2 minutes—under the 3-minute Service Level Agreement (SLA) they set in peak times—not only acknowledging her problem and frustration, but fully resolving the issue in the original Messenger conversation in a fraction of the time it would have taken on the phone. Because of the outstanding service, Sarah messaged the company saying:

"I'm rather stunned actually. Corporations and businesses don't very often react to human problems in a human way, so consider our relationship repaired. And in the interests of fairness I will spread news of your kindness if you don't object. I think it is a genuinely wonderful thing to do and I wasn't expecting a reply, let alone this."[11]

The modern consumer has a voice, has a choice, and they are in charge. The question is: are they going to use their megaphone for brand building, as Sarah did; or brand bombing, as Mr. Syed did? The answer lies in how brands engage and treat consumers on digital and social channels. Figuring out how best to serve the modern customer starts with understanding how the modern customer has changed.

CONSUMERS HAVE A VOICE AND A CHOICE

"People are using their role as influential consumers on Twitter to reach out directly and expect to have a dialog with a brand. It changes the game when the conversation starts out in a public arena. Customers are effectively holding brands accountable for a great care experience."

— Chris Moody, GM Data & Enterprise Solutions at Twitter

One of the defining characteristics of the modern consumer is the extent to which they are in control of the message. They have a voice across messaging channels with their immediate friends and family and they have a voice with total strangers across public social media platforms (as evidenced by Hasan Syed's promoted tweet).

There has been a steady drumbeat over the years of new options for consumers to seek service and express themselves. Originally, it was in-person and by letter. Then, the telephone came along and the toll-free "hotline" changed everything. The space between complaint and contact center shrank. With the rise of the Internet came email, then web chat. These channels made it easier than ever before for customers to ask for help (but not necessarily to get an answer and real resolution in the time-frame or in the place that they needed it).

Alongside this channel explosion brands implemented rigid and structured scripting to ensure consistency and reputation management. Agents were coached how best to answer the phone and email to minimize mistakes and protect the brand. Too often, getting help meant navigating complex phone trees and then repeatedly asking for a manager before finding someone who can actually help—we entered the world of "computer says no."[12]

Then came social media.

Social media forced brands to change their service model. Issues happening across social channels are broadcast for all to see. It's the airing of dirty laundry writ large. In the general population, someone who has a good service experience will tell 15 people, while someone who has a bad service experience will tell 24 people. But among social media users, people will share their positive experiences with 42 people, and their bad experiences with 53 people.[13] That's over twice as many as non-social media users. For the customer service leader, the fact that consumers now control the choice of channel—for either compliment or complaint—is what provides both the most opportunity and the most peril. With execs stressing about the potential negative impact of a social media incident—just note the drop in United's share price after the video of a man being dragged off a plane by Chicago police went viral—service teams have done as much as possible to ensure they are staying on top of any potential issues, while struggling to figure out how social fits into their wider customer service strategy.

CONSUMERS WITH COMPLAINTS ARE GOING TO SOCIAL MESSAGING FIRST

Social customer service started as an escalation channel. Consumers would use the public nature of social media to try and get resolution when they had already suffered a bad experience elsewhere, or were struggling to get an answer fast enough over more traditional channels—tweeting while they were also on the phone or waiting for an email response. But with the rise of private messaging, and increasing consumer awareness that issues can be resolved faster through these channels (often with a direct line to a more flexible agent, empowered to resolve issues quickly by whatever means necessary), consumers increasingly choose to go to social messaging channels first.

> ## 54% of customers prefer social messaging channels for care over phone/email, and 35% of 18–34 year olds use social media for customer care regularly.
>
> —Conversocial Social Effort Study[14]

CONSUMERS FIND SOCIAL MEDIA AND MESSAGING THE EASIEST CHANNELS FOR SERVICE

Think of the last time you tweeted a company to ask a question. Why did you do it? I do this frequently—because it's easy. I don't have to look up a support email address. I don't have to wait on hold. I don't have to sit at my desktop in a chat session. I just pull out my phone and fire off a question.

In a study by Aspect Research, consumers rated service over Twitter as 2 times less frustrating than email, and 5 times less frustrating than phone—similar findings to when BT implemented their "Net Easy" scores, and found social care easier to use than phone by 4:1, and easier than email and self-service by 2:1. And when Conversocial surveyed a representative sample of American consumers in 2016, 45% of respondents said that "Ease of Use" was the most important aspect of social customer service.[15] 42% of respondents preferred social media for service issues because it allowed them to multitask while awaiting issue resolution and proved more convenient. This ease and convenience for customers is one of the biggest drivers of the growth of social and messaging for service, and the resulting impact on customer loyalty is a major benefit to companies who promote it.

Twitter is 2x less frustrating than email, and 5x less frustrating than phone. (Aspect Research)[16]

THE MODERN CONSUMER LIVES IN THE MOMENT

We live in a real-time world. When something newsworthy hits Twitter, it spreads around the world faster than wildfire. When we as individuals are doing something even vaguely interesting or amusing we're Snapchatting it, Instagramming it, or live-streaming it over Facebook Live or Periscope to our friends. We get real time updates on when our taxi will arrive, when our food will be here, and when our Amazon Prime Now (ordered only 20 minutes ago) will be delivered. Even when watching a live game on TV, half our attention is on our "second screen" to be part of the real-time conversation happening online.

In this real-time world, when consumers experience a question or service issue, they expect to be able to get an answer there and then, in that moment of need. Are you willing to wait on hold anymore? Are you satisfied with an email 24 hours after you had a problem? The concept of service and support needs to align to this in-the-moment lifestyle that is powered by powerful smartphones. For the customer, *the moment of need* is all that matters.

The other reality of this world is that a brand is only as good as their last in-the-moment service interaction, and nowhere is this more powerful than in the airline industry. A customer who experienced stellar service aboard an 18-hour flight whose bags have gone missing on arrival only cares about when her bags are going to show up. In this situation, a quick response from an airline can defuse the situation and keep the customer happy—but the clock is ticking.

According to the research that Conversocial conducted on the Twitter response speed of major airlines across the US and Europe,[17] a passenger tweeting Alaska Airlines will get a response in an average of 2 minutes and 34 seconds. But if they tweet at one of the slowest airlines in the report, they can expect a response anywhere from one and a half hours to *five hours and 48 minutes after initial contact.*

Which experience engenders loyalty and word-of-mouth praise? Expectations for in-the-moment resolution are not confined to the airline industry. They are set by the organizations delivering top tier service and experiences across every industry: an Alaska Airlines customer asking an ecommerce brand why their delivery is late now expects a 3-minute response time as well.

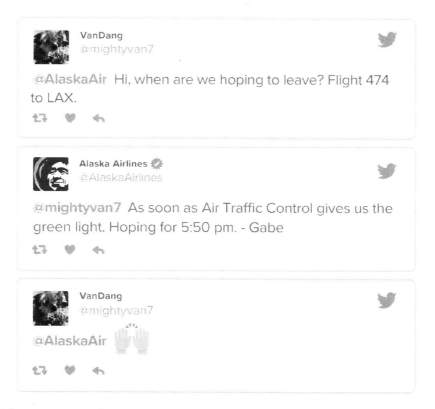

There were just three minutes from when the customer (sitting on tarmac) tweeted this question to when Alaska Airlines responded.

CASE STUDY: DELL'S APPROACH TO SOCIAL CUSTOMER SERVICE

On June 21, 2005, a citizen journalist named Jeff Jarvis posted an extremely negative blog post about his customer service experience with the giant computer technology company Dell, painstakingly documenting his ongoing customer service troubles after purchasing a dud laptop. His blog post went viral, and ended up being picked up by the *New York Times*, then *Business Week*. It went from a single angry customer to a public relations firestorm. The story sounds familiar today—companies are hit by similar issues almost every week. But this was before the advent of Facebook and Twitter, before "United Breaks Guitars," and before the Arab Spring.

At the time, companies didn't realize the power of social media, and hadn't been paying attention. But this situation made Dell one of the first companies to sit up and take action. They put a 14-year company veteran, Lionel Menchaca, in charge of their blog and started a real dialogue with customers. In the blog posts following the incident, Menchaca was open in admitting the problems that the company had, and responded publicly to bloggers and customers. According to Jarvis, Manchaca gave the company "a human voice." Manchaca gave customers respect and "got respect in return. It works."[18]

Fast forward to 2017, and Dell is still one of the leading social companies, from their CEO Michael Dell (who is personally engaged on Twitter) down. Dell has gone from a small listening outpost and blog to having over 300 social customer service agents, making them one of the biggest social care operations globally. Social is no longer a separate division, but is deeply integrated into the fabric of how Dell operates.

Alison Herzog is the Director of Global Social Business at Dell, reporting into the Chief Customer Office. After a twenty-year career touching various aspects of the customer experience, she joined Dell as it was completing its acquisition of EMC (the largest tech acquisition of all time) in order to lead the social business integration of the two technology behemoths. Following the success of this integration, Dell opened the Chief Customer Office to have a team who sat across all business divisions, and ensured everyone across the giant company was working together for the benefit of the end-customer. Alison's remit is to ensure that the way that social media is handled—across marketing, customer service, and sales—all fits together seamlessly for the benefit of customers and the business.

This is especially complex for Dell, which not only has a large consumer business, but also runs a large and complex B2B business—two worlds that can frequently collide: "Recently the CIO of a major company we work with tweeted us with a customer care question about his daughter's laptop. We were able to see that this wasn't just a normal consumer and triaged it immediately to the right escalation office to make sure that it was handled appropriately."

This requires continuous work to ensure they have integration across tech stacks and across the different identifiers for their customers. This doesn't mean that only their B2B customers get the best service—just that they need to ensure they have a unified approach. Alison says: "All customers matter if you reach out to Dell Cares: we have an SLA of one hour for public messages and an SLA of four hours for private messages. It doesn't matter who you are, we are going to try to respond to you as quickly as possible and we hold ourselves accountable to these SLAs regardless of status."

Alison is also a big proponent of the concept of effort in customer service: "In our day and age, we are used to just being able to get what we want very quickly. When we tweet at a company we want it to be as seamless as possible. I think it's really important for brands to focus on how they can make the experience as simple as possible, and not require a lot of different steps. We want things to be as easy as possible."

Looking ahead, Dell is looking into how AI and automation can be used to improve the customer experience, and make service exchanges easier and simpler: "If I can send a private message or direct message and say, 'Hey, I'm having a problem with such and such,' AI should be able to either quickly answer my question or put it in the right queue for an agent. Even these simple things create huge opportunities—the more we can leverage automation for agents, the more it frees up our resources to be able to help folks who really need to speak to a human, such as if it's a more complex issue."

But within this, maintaining a human brand which aligns with customers' values will always be important: "I think the trend is going to be not only having to have a differentiated customer experience in sales, marketing and service—but that also you are a human brand that cares and makes a difference. It's something that we do a great job of. That's why I love Dell."

KEY TAKEAWAYS

- Any negative service experience is just one tweet away from going viral, with potentially damning impact on your brand (and stock price).

- Although social care started with the public escalation of issues from other service channels, it's increasingly the first choice for consumers.

- Social media and mobile messaging are the easiest channels for your customers to use for customer service—meaning they are least likely to reduce customer loyalty after any service interaction.

- Leading companies commit to full resolution of issues over social media, in minutes—that's the expectation all your customers have today.

CHAPTER 3
The Rise of Messaging

• •

Today, if you start a new business in China, you don't put up a website first—you open an official WeChat account. WeChat is the web.

—Ted Livingston, CEO, Kik[19]

On February 24th, 2009, Jan Koum incorporated WhatsApp Inc. in California, and began developing what would become the biggest messaging app in the world within just a few years. WhatsApp started as a basic way to send status updates to all the friends in your phone address book—but as people started to use this as a way to send messages to their friends, Koum realized that he'd inadvertently created a messaging service. As Koum said, "being able to reach somebody half way across the world instantly, on a device that is always with you, was powerful."

At the time, mobile messaging meant SMS, which was expensive—especially to other countries. There was BBM, but that only worked between BlackBerries. And although Skype was free, that required creating a completely new social graph. WhatsApp was uniquely simple in that the login was your own phone number, and you could instantly connect with everyone in your phone book. After they released WhatsApp 2.0 on the iPhone with messaging built in, their user base quickly grew to over a quarter of a million people. They started to get a flood of requests to launch on other platforms, so that their iPhone users could message friends on Nokias and Blackberries around the world for free. They got to work on expanding the platforms, and by 2011 they were firmly in the top 20 of all apps in the U.S. App Store. By 2013, WhatsApp's user base had grown to 200 million people around the world. By 2014, that had grown to 450 million, with a million more joining every day.

On February 19th, 2014, Facebook bought WhatsApp for $19 billion.

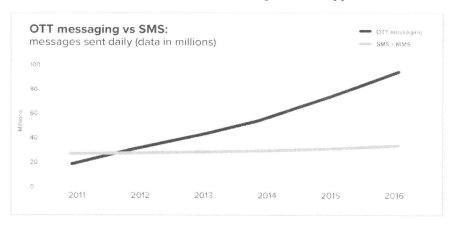

The growth of "Over the Top" (OTT) messaging, sent over data, vs SMS and MMS volumes.[20]

WHY ALL THE FUSS?

Messaging is more than just a way of sending free text messages to your friends. It's also a different communication paradigm compared to other digital channels, like email. Some of the key defining characteristics of messaging:

- Mobile-first, so people expect short, concise messages—and a fast response time

- Rich media (photos, videos, gifs) are part of the conversation

- Conversations are arranged around *people* (not *subjects* like email), with the people, brands or groups you've spoken to most recently closest to the top. When you enter into a conversation, it's a continuous thread, and if you haven't messaged someone for a while the full history of all of your messages between each other will still be right there.

Today, messaging hasn't just eclipsed SMS in most countries. Messaging apps (including Facebook Messenger, WhatsApp, WeChat in Asia, Snapchat, and more) have also eclipsed social networks, in both total users and growth rates. Facebook Messenger took roughly 40 months to reach 500 million users, then doubled to 1 billion users just 20 months later, an incredible achievement.[21] WeChat skyrocketed from 100 million monthly active users to 500 million in just a year and a half.[22] Today, six out of the ten most used apps on iTunes and Google Play are messaging apps.

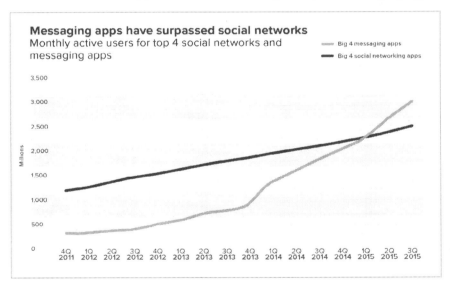

The growth in user base of the biggest four messaging apps vs. the biggest four social networking apps. Source: Business Insider Intelligence[23]

THE DEATH OF PHONE AND EMAIL

Phone calls and email are dead for the next generation. Social media and mobile messaging completely dominate how teenagers today use their phones, as you can see from Ofcom's comparison of phone usage for Adults versus Teens in the UK. This is a glimpse into the future—if you think your customers hate having to call and wait on hold today, the customers of tomorrow will be livid. Which brands do you think these customers will want to buy from: ones that engage and interact in the same way they communicate all the time, or ones that force them into old channels that are high effort and (for them) unusual?

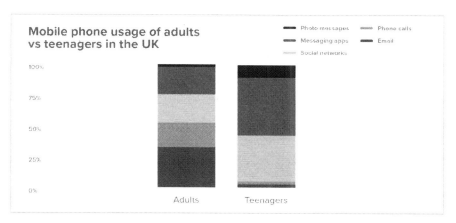

Mobile phone usage of adults vs. teenagers in the UK show that messaging and social networks have completely eclipsed phone and email. Source: Ofcom (UK)

This isn't just teenagers though—as the Ofcom data show, almost half of adult mobile phone usage today is with social and messaging apps, a trend that is strongest with the millennial generation[24] (which now ranges up to people in their mid-thirties). The messaging platforms are already dominant in terms of both overall communication channels and application usage, and these patterns are becoming more ingrained with each passing month, year, and generation.

FROM SUBJECTS TO PEOPLE

Messaging is a different paradigm of communication. In email—the predominant legacy digital communication medium—messages (both 1:1 and between multiple people), and the replies to those messages, are all organized by subject line. Subject lines and the to/from/cc fields can also change, which can easily create confusion and difficulty in following conversations. In messaging, communication is organized around a continuous conversation with a person, a group of people, or a brand. It's much more intuitive. People can organize their life around people, and brands can organize interactions around customers. It's a more natural and intuitive way to manage your communication.

This people-based way of managing communication has become a dominant force in all walks of life. It's how modern SMS and messaging work. It's how messaging apps like Facebook Messenger and WhatsApp work. And, it has started to become dominant at work with apps like Slack and HipChat. It has become the dominant communication archetype for how individuals interact with each other in any digital context. In fact, Slack, which brought consumer-like messaging to the enterprise, has been one of the fastest growing B2B companies ever, with a growth rate almost as fast as the consumer messaging applications.

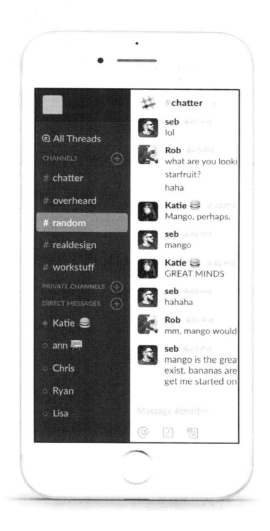

A screenshot of Slack, a messaging app for the enterprise, which works seam-lessly across mobile, web and desktop applications, and organizes communication around people and groups—not subjects.

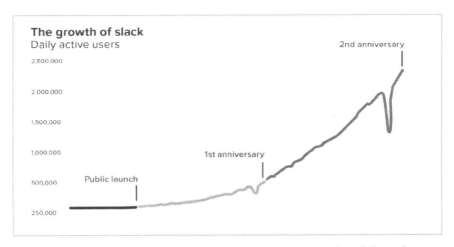

The growth of slack
Daily active users

2nd anniversary

2,500,000

2,000,000

1,500,000

1,000,000

1st anniversary

500,000 — Public launch

250,000

The growth of slack, an enterprise messaging application, has followed a similar growth trajectory to consumer messaging apps.[25]

In today's world of information overload where everyone is drowning in email, this people-centric organizational paradigm is more efficient, easier to manage, and more likely to elicit a response. It's a more human-centric, streamlined way of communicating that makes it easier for people to stay on top of things and is more relevant to how we think about the world. The main platform players have recognized this shift and quickly moved to offer messaging apps, whether it's interactive messaging on top of SMS like Apple iMessage, or WhatsApp which has replaced SMS in most of the world. And the trend is only going to accelerate given how the next generation use digital platforms to communicate.

THE SHIFT FROM PUBLIC SOCIAL TO PRIVATE MESSAGING

Although social media customer care started in response to public complaints on Twitter and Facebook, for many brands the majority of questions and complaints have now shifted to private messaging channels. I observed this shift happen for many of the biggest brands Conversocial works with in 2016. A key factor is that this shift happens for brands who are actively promoting their private channels for service—brands who don't do this continue to get a high volume of public complaints. *Promoting social care in the right way will actually decrease the amount of complaints about you on Twitter!*

Promoting social care in the right way will actually decrease the amount of complaints about you on Twitter!

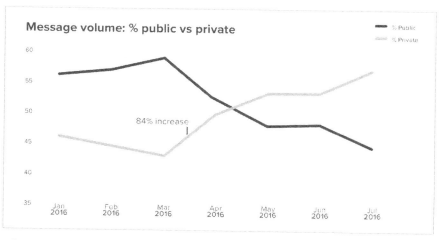

Message volume: % public vs private

- % Public
- % Private

84% increase

The volume of public vs. private messages at selection of major brands who work with Conversocial in 2016, showing the shift in incoming volume from public to private messages.

On Twitter, this shift has been helped not only by the ability to directly promote "DM Us" buttons in websites and apps, but also by new features that Twitter built within the platform, including "Send a private message" buttons in public conversations, and new larger "Message Us" buttons on Twitter profile pages.

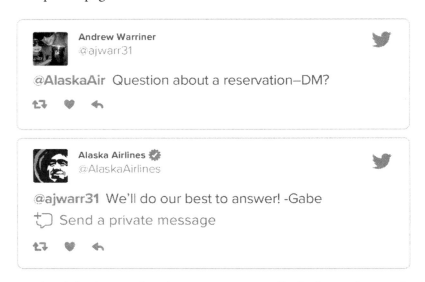

Example of the button "Send a private message" which can be seamlessly appended to a public Twitter conversation to take it into private messaging.

Example of Twitter's new profile page for businesses, which includes large "Message" buttons.

It's now easy to promote private messaging with buttons for your websites and mobile apps that link directly to Messenger and Twitter DMs, and the benefits in terms of reduced public complaints and decreased effort for customer are huge. One Conversocial customer who has been promoting "Message Us" buttons on their website, mobile app and emails for the last two years now receives 98% of all their inbound Facebook volume *privately,* with only a tiny amount of public posts. For companies who are concerned that promoting social care will increase public complaints, this data shows that the exact opposite will happen.

THE USE OF MESSAGING APPS FOR SERVICE

On March 25, 2015, at their annual developer conference F8, Facebook officially launched "Messenger for Business," opening up a live-chat API with a group of select partners. I was there at the launch along with our client, Hyatt Hotels, who was one of the first partners to launch live-chat over Messenger. In the months following the announcement, dozens, then hundreds, then thousands of major brands began using Messenger to deliver customer service.

Messaging combines full live-chat functionality with persistent identity and mobile notifications—combining all of the best elements of the traditional digital care channels, purpose-built for the mobile era:

- Real-time (many messaging applications even show when the other person is typing)

- Asynchronous (you can go away and continue the conversation later)

- Persistent identity (and easy to link to a customer record)

- Connected to smartphone notifications

Although businesses had been using the private messaging functionality of Facebook Pages and Twitter accounts for years, the lack of real-time messaging and typing indicators meant that this operated more like email, and wasn't as useful for in-the-moment service. The new functionality inside Messenger (and shortly afterward, available in Twitter as well) also included the ability to add basic automation, giving more businesses a reason to switch over.

The combination of functionality available to businesses in modern messaging apps makes them extremely convenient for consumers to use for service (just pull out your phone and send a message), with big benefits for businesses in terms of efficiency. If they are confident they will get a real-time response to their issues, consumers will message instead of phoning. This makes messaging the first digital care channel that has the potential to replace a significant percentage of phone calls—something that will have a massively positive impact on the customer experience while decreasing the high costs that businesses spend on phone calls every year.

CASE STUDY: PROMOTING MESSAGING AT YOUNIQUE

Younique is a beauty products company that was founded in September 2012 by a brother-and-sister team, Derek Maxfield and Melanie Huscroft. Combining the traditional home party business model with the ability to hold virtual parties online, it grew rapidly to serve over 4 million customers, and was valued at over a billion dollars in 2016, when Coty Inc. (who own CoverGirl makeup and Clairol hair dye) bought a majority stake.

After starting to operationalize customer care over social media and mobile messaging, Younique realized that Facebook Messenger was not only the most convenient way for their customers to get help—but was also cheaper and more effective than traditional service channels. They use the live-chat functionality of Messenger to provide real time service and support when customers reach out.

On March 21st, they made the switch to start promoting Messenger as the primary customer service channel on their website. In just two months, they saw an 877% increase in private messages, a huge jump—while emails and chats dropped accordingly. They also saw a 52% drop in public social media comments, with service posts disappearing almost entirely from their Facebook pages.

Younique's support page, which promotes Facebook Messenger as their primary support channel.

Messaging, in whatever form it takes, is the first always-on, real-time service channel on your mobile device which has the potential to radically shift service volume away from phone calls while dramatically reducing friction and the service cost structure.

Messaging, in whatever form it takes, is the first always-on, real-time service channel on your mobile device which has the potential to radically shift service volume away from phone calls while dramatically reducing friction and the service cost structure.

Messaging platforms aren't just about a new paradigm for live-chat, however. They've also started to enable rich, interactive functionality to build bots and other automated experiences. We explore this development in the next chapter.

KEY TAKEAWAYS

- Messaging has been the fastest growing communication paradigm for both consumers and businesses, and will only continue to grow in dominance.

- Messaging is centered around real-time, continuous conversations with people—not subjects.

- Social care is now more about private messaging than public escalation—and if you promote private messaging, you'll decrease the amount of public complaints you receive.

- Messaging combines the benefits of live chat with the benefits of email, in a mobile-first platform that all your customers have in their pocket. It's the first digital service channel with the potential to fully replace phone calls—and companies are successfully deflecting volumes from traditional channels to messaging today.

CHAPTER 4

The Year of the Bots

⦁ ⦁

Chatbots represent a new trend in how people access information, make decisions, and communicate. We think that chatbots are the beginning of a new form of digital access, which centers on messaging.

—Christie Pitts, Ventures Development Manager at Verizon Ventures

Elizabeth Johnson is a busy working mom who wants to book a makeover. She unexpectedly has the next Monday off because her team delivered a big project ahead of schedule so she decided to treat herself. Since she spends most of her digital life messaging coworkers and friends on platforms such as Slack and Messenger, she decided to visit Sephora on Messenger—and was greeted with a notice saying "Hi! If you'd like to speak to a customer service representative, select that option below. You can also easily book a makeover with the Sephora Reservation Assistant by selecting 'Book now.'"

Bingo, she thought. *I have just enough time to book the appointment before meeting a friend for coffee.* She selected 11 a.m. on Monday, her day off, then entered her city and swiped through two nearby stores. She remembered she'd be doing some errands the next town over and changed the city. The automated reservation assistant sent her a confirmation message and the entire process, including changes, took less than two minutes—all on a platform she was already using with friends, without needing to download anything else. *Wow, that was easy*, she thought, as she moved on to check her messages on Slack.

Seamlessly addressing customer needs on a mobile phone, using a messaging app, at the moment of need, is one of the hallmarks of where the future of service is heading. But while there have been many examples of funny or amusing bots, many of the attempts at more serious bots for sales or service have been badly built and a poor user experience. However, there are a small but increasing number that, like the Sephora bot, are adding real value and making customers' lives easier. Shane Mac, the CEO of bot platform provider Assist (which built the Sephora bot) noted:

> In every other instance, when you're talking to a Sephora agent on the phone and you say, "I'd like to book an appointment at 11. Actually, can I do 1 p.m. instead?" the system works because it's a human you're talking to. Well, our technology does that too. It allows you to change your mind so the customer is never mad or stuck in this endless loop of "Sorry, I don't understand. That's not the question I was asking you." It's just starting to get to the point where we're applying the technology in a much better way than it was in the past to specific use cases, making the customer a lot happier.

The products being built by Mac's team at Assist are the vanguard of a new wave of bots inside messaging apps built for speed, convenience, and ease-of-use. This new breed of convenient interactive functionality makes the lives of Elizabeth Johnson and millions of other customers easier by rapidly executing specific, high value tasks or service solutions. As Mr. Mac noted when asked about metrics for success, "Reducing friction is our only metric."

2016: THE BOT HYPE CYCLE

Chris Messina is a well-known and visionary engineer who is credited with the invention of the #hashtag. He proposed using them to manage groups on Twitter back in 2007—but Twitter originally rejected the idea, thinking that #hashtags were too nerdy[26] and wouldn't catch on (later, after users *did* start using them regularly, they adopted them as official functionality).

In January 2016, while he was working at Uber, Chris Messina wrote a visionary blog post that quickly went viral across the tech world: "2016 will be the year of conversational commerce."[27] A huge believer in the ability for automated conversations—delivered over messaging—to replace applications, he made a number of bold predictions on the upcoming shift in how we would all be interacting with brands.

One of his big predictions—that Facebook would make major moves in the space—came true on April 12th 2016, at Facebook's annual developer conference F8. I was sitting close to the front row when Mark Zuckerberg came on stage. Outside of developments they were making in Virtual Reality, the biggest announcement was the launch of their bot platform. This allowed developers to build automated experiences in Messenger that included not just conversations, but also interactive elements such as images, menu buttons, and carousels.

Mark Zuckerberg on stage at F8 in 2016, announcing the launch of the Messenger Platform. (photo by the author)

The launch of the Facebook Messenger platform was followed by big announcements around "bot" platforms and developer tools in various forms by Twitter, Microsoft, Google, Amazon, and more. The press went crazy. The headlines heralded a new future of AI-driven automation touching every aspect of our lives. All commerce in the future was to be conversational and delivered through messaging. All human service agents would be replaced by bots. Every mobile app would be instantly replaced by a bot.

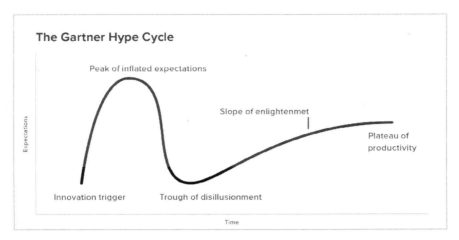

The Gartner Hype Cycle

Peak of inflated expectations

Slope of enlightenmet

Plateau of productivity

Innovation trigger

Trough of disillusionment

Expectations

Time

Gartner Hype Cycle[28]

It was incredible to watch the perception of bots go through the hype cycle stages at warp speed. It felt like we hit the "Peak of Inflated Expectations" in a matter of weeks, before falling almost as quickly into the "Trough of Disillusionment" (according to my own analysis, not Gartner). The new Messenger platform and related announcements made it easier to build interactive experiences—but they didn't push forward the state of AI or conversational bots. Brands and third-party developers still had to build the intelligence behind the bots, and this hadn't gotten any easier because of the launch of the bot platforms.

So the announcements, although exciting for the platforms, weren't as exciting for users—most of the bots that were released were very basic, and a terrible user experience. Some chatbots (like Microsoft's Taybot, on Twitter) bombed so badly they had to be taken down. Almost all the bots being built by developers and brands were simply using basic, rule-based decision trees that worked fine for simple transactions, but would quickly frustrate a customer looking for help with anything off-script—and, the hand-off between bots and humans on these platforms hadn't been developed, creating yet more confusion and frustration.

The fact is, rule-based chat bots have been around for decades—and although they have some limited value, in most cases companies gave up on them because they just lead to frustrating customer experiences. Given that human-powered chat is cheaper to provide than a phone call, why create a negative automated chat experience that could just result in the customer phoning anyway? With this background, launching rule-based chat bots into messaging didn't seem to be that valuable a proposition.

ADDING REAL VALUE: TRANSACTIONAL BOTS

Despite the hype and the crash, there is one type of bot that has been a clear winner for both businesses and users. By using the new interactive functionality within Messenger (buttons, carousels, pictures etc.), it is possible to offer simple transactional experiences (like the Sephora booking app) that are extremely convenient and easy for customers to use, delivering greater ease-of-use than with a pure "conversational UI," without the customer needing to download a fully dedicated application for the brand. These kind of bots—enabling customers to order flowers, change flights, or book a hotel room, for example—if paired to go alongside human agents, with seamless handoff, can drive real value for brands in terms of increased revenue and decreased costs, all while delivering a more effortless experience for the customer.

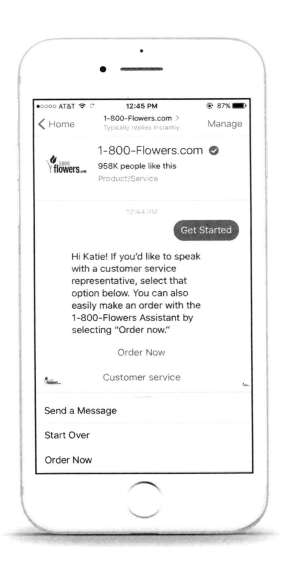

The 1-800-Flowers.com Messenger bot makes it easy to order flowers without having to download a standalone app.

WHERE THIS ALL STARTED: WECHAT

The first consumer messaging platform to really integrate businesses and transactions was WeChat in China, which combined messaging with a fully featured app and transaction platform. According to Connie Chan from venture capital firm Andreessen Horowitz, WeChat is fundamentally rethinking the role messaging can play:

"Philosophically, while Facebook and WhatsApp measure growth by the number of daily and monthly active users on their networks, WeChat cares more about how relevant and central WeChat is in addressing the daily, even hourly needs of its users. Instead of focusing on building the largest social network in the world, WeChat has focused on building a mobile lifestyle—its goal is to address every aspect of its users' lives, including non-social ones."[29]

Official accounts on WeChat are built to execute tasks as diverse as ordering a taxi, paying a utility bill, making a doctor appointment, ordering food for delivery, or buying movie tickets—all from within the messaging app.

In the search for how to bring businesses into messaging and start to monetize the platform, Facebook Messenger looked to the WeChat model for inspiration. However, there are some important differences: brands build mini-applications inside WeChat, not conversational bot experiences; and, WeChat developed in the "Wild East" of China, which was experiencing rapid consumer growth in mobile on a set of very diverse, low cost Android platforms that didn't have a consistent app store or user experience. In that background, a consistent WeChat platform proved essential for businesses. In the more mature app environment in the West, messaging platforms have a lot more to prove.

McDonalds "mini-program" in WeChat, devoted to coupons. This is more like a mini application or website—not a conversational bot.

THE SHIFT FROM APPS TO BOTS

In most cases, transactional bots (like the one for 1-800-Flowers.com) can't replace human agents for service issues. But they do have the potential to replace dedicated applications for businesses. Dedicated branded apps, while powerful, require heavy investment (costing a lot to produce and maintain for all the different devices and app stores). More importantly, native apps are generally only downloaded and used by your most dedicated customers. Unless you're an app-based business like Lyft or Uber, the vast majority of your customers will either never download or never use your own branded applications. Messaging applications, on the other hand, are used by all of your customers today—and now enable you to deliver interactive experiences to them instantly.

David Marcus, VP of Messaging for Facebook, explained the company's vision for how brands can use bots and messaging to deliver better experiences:

> We have an opportunity between mobile websites and apps to build a new space which doesn't require the download of an app and we feel that we have an opportunity because messaging persists identity, and especially Messenger, because we have the identity of Facebook which is a real identity.

> So take the case of airlines, for instance. We have airlines that are now building experiences on Messenger. When you build your airline tickets you get your itinerary on Messenger. When it's time to check in you get a notification. You have that nice bubble with a button that says check in. You get your boarding pass. If you are stuck in traffic you can just say "I'm not going to make it. Put me on the next flight." And the idea of not having to identify yourself but having the ability to interact with all the brands and services without having to re-establish context every time is a game changer for people and for business alike.[30]

With billions of users, a constantly improving platform, and a low cost of entry (compared to dedicated applications), any business looking to deliver transactional experiences to their customers should be building bots on both Messenger and Twitter. Later on we'll look at what kind of bot experiences you should be building today, and which you should avoid.

KEY TAKEAWAYS

- After the announcement of multiple bot platforms, there was a lot of hype—but although there is a lot of potential, stand-alone "bots" are only useful in a few limited use cases.

- The biggest winner is using messaging bots for simple transactions, such as ordering flowers, making reservations or booking a hotel room. These are simple and more effortless than requiring a customer to download a dedicated application.

- This represents a wider shift from downloading a full-fledged branded application to instead having relevant functionality delivered instantly over messaging at the point of need.

CHAPTER 5

Developments in AI

• •

As an industry, we are on the cusp of a new frontier that pairs the power of natural human language with advanced machine intelligence.

—Satya Nadella, Microsoft CEO[31]

When I was growing up, while many of my contemporaries were learning chess, I was instead fascinated by the ancient Asian board game 'Go'. A huge part of this fascination came from the fact that, until 2016, no computer had ever beaten a professional Go player—whereas the best human chess player of all time, Gary Kasparov, had been beaten by the IBM computer "Deep Blue" in 1997. I still occasionally go to my local Go club, near my apartment in New York (where I'm usually the weakest player).

In the early days of AI development, chess programs had been looked to as an example of how a computer could, one day, learn to think like humans. However, scientists quickly found out that the best way to build a chess program didn't include much intelligence at all. Instead, they could use "brute force" techniques that would calculate, one at a time, the potential outcome of every possible move. Even though these decision trees could go into the millions, the increasing speed of computers meant that every year the chess programs got better and better, until by 1997 they were unbeatable.

Whereas chess has a relatively narrow degree of freedom (a limited set of pieces with a limited set of allowable moves in each turn), Go—with 361 squares on the board, and pieces able to move on any of them every turn—has many more degrees of freedom. Because of this, even the fastest computers using a "brute force" technique were unable to play at the level of professional Go players. Instead, Go served for decades as a bellwether of computers' ability to use AI techniques to "pattern match," to learn from data to recognize situations and appropriate actions—like humans do—without needing to calculate every single move individually.

The bellwether for AI chimed on March 15th 2016 at the Four Seasons Hotel in Seoul, during the conclusion of the Go match between "AlphaGo," the Go program developed by Google's DeepMind division, and Lee Sedol, the 18-time Go world champion. AlphaGo won.

Unlike Deep Blue's brute force algorithms, AlphaGo used neural networks that were trained on millions of moves from real games, then continually played against itself and used reinforcement learning to improve its own play. As one of the AlphaGo creators explained:[32]

"Although we have programmed this machine to play, we have no idea what moves it will come up with. Its moves are an emergent phenomenon from the training. We just create the data sets and the training algorithms. But the moves it then comes up with are out of our hands—and much better than we, as Go players, could come up with."

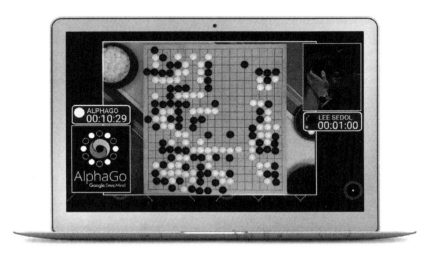

AlphaGo playing Lee Sedol in one of the Go games AlphaGo won, beating the top human player for the first time in history.

WHAT DO PEOPLE MEAN WHEN THEY SAY "AI"?

Artificial intelligence is an umbrella term housing many advanced techniques, algorithms, computational methods, and mathematical models that are proving useful at predicting outcomes, identifying service issues, recognizing faces, recommending movies, categorizing data, and translating speech. All of these techniques are also considered machine learning: in popular usage, AI is often used to describe use cases that haven't yet been built, while machine learning is used for techniques in common usage.

The classical notion of AI—think Hal 9000, a robot able to think, talk, and learn much like a human—is known as "General" or "Strong" AI. Popularized by science fiction, right now this remains just that—fiction. We still don't have a great understanding of how general human intelligence works, and even bullish experts believe we are still 30 years away from achieving this kind of general AI.

"Narrow," or "Weak" AI is the kind that we are starting to see in everyday life. This is the application of machine learning techniques to a specific field or discrete problem that needs to be solved. AlphaGo is amazing at playing Go—but if you asked it a question in English, or tried to get it to drive a car, it would have no idea how to respond. On the other hand, Tesla's autopilot can now self-drive Teslas on highways, can spot other cars and obstacles, and knows the rules of the road—but couldn't play Go.

In recent years, the application of narrow AI has been getting more and more useful. From self-driving cars to Alexa understanding our speech, computers are more and more able to understand natural input and interact in the real world. The error rates in many useful areas such as image recognition, speech recognition, and natural language processing have fallen to close to human rates.

What's changed?

"First we need to enable machines to understand intent from natural language a lot better. The services that we now power for airlines, for luxury brands and for all kinds of different services are powered by AI to some extent because we help them to extract intent from conversation and as a result automate a lot of those interactions."[33]

- David Marcus, Facebook VP of Messaging

THE EMERGENCE OF DEEP LEARNING

AlphaGo's learning abilities, Tesla's self-driving cars, and Alexa's speech understanding are rather diverse talents. It may come as a surprise, then, that they are all powered by a single approach: Deep Learning. Deep Learning leverages research into statistical models that are inspired by biological brain cells (and the connections between these cells). While an individual "artificial neuron" is a very simple algorithm, they become powerful and widely useful when many of them—thousands, or in some uses, millions—are connected together into a network.

When artificial neurons are stacked more than three layers high this is definitionally a Deep Learning neural network. The first layer takes in data, does some simple calculations and feeds the processed data into the second layer. After further simple processing, the second layer passes data along into the third, and so on. With each successive layer, the neurons represent increasingly abstract derivations of the data. As an example, the first layer of a neural network trained to recognize faces will become adept at detecting outlines; the middle layers will become specialized at identifying elements of faces (e. g., lips, noses, eyes); and the highest layers will tie all these representations together to distinguish whole faces.

A deep neural net can be fed large quantities of data, and is able to learn patterns in the input data (e.g., the edges and eyes that make up a face), eliminating the need for humans to spell these out explicitly. The system continues to learn and get better over time with each cycle of data inputted. Computer scientists can teach a Deep Learning algorithm to do repetitive actions to categorize, predict, and recommend based on crunching enormous sets of data, without ever needing to give the system any information about what that data is.

The concepts behind Deep Learning and Neural Nets have been around for many decades, with the first working algorithm for Deep Learning published in 1957.[34] The current leaders in Deep Learning research have been publishing research on neural nets for nearly three decades—Yann LeCun, director of AI research for Facebook, published a paper titled "Shortest path segmentation: A method for training a neural network to recognize character strings" in 1992.[35] That's 25 years ago.

However, for most practical use cases of Deep Learning you need enormous data sets. Even if you could get hold of enough data, putting huge data sets through multilevel neural nets was prohibitively expensive and slow 20 or even 10 years ago. As a result, AI research focused on other machine learning techniques that were less computationally expensive, but were more laborious for humans to implement—because more processing and categorization of the input data was required before these machine learning algorithms could be applied. In contrast to the Deep Learning case where features (e.g., face outlines and eyes) can be learned from the raw data, the researchers needed to tell the algorithm which features to learn from. It's only in recent years that easy access to large data volumes and inexpensive, fast, and powerful computing finally combined with 60 years of Deep Learning thinking and algorithm development to create breakthroughs.

BIG (CAT) DATA

Soft-spoken and straightforward, Andrew Ng earned his Master's degree from M.I.T and his PhD from UC Berkeley. He recently left a post as VP and Chief Scientist for Baidu, the Chinese search and internet services company. But it was his work as part of the Google Brain project in 2012 that sent a shot across the bow of computer scientists (and YouTube lovers) the world over.

Ng and his team, including Jeff Dean who leads Google Brain, wanted to see if they could use Deep Learning techniques to feed a computer a huge amount of data—over 10 million YouTube videos—and see what it could learn to categorize inside the videos (faces, bridges, cars, cats etc.) without being told what to search for or what items were present in the data. Like a child learning to recognize facial patterns before being able to speak, can the computer learn what's in the data on its own?

The "Cat Paper" as it came to be known was a milestone in the field of narrow artificial intelligence (AI) because it was a compelling example how scientists could quickly apply an algorithm to a massive data set in a way that clearly showed computers could "learn" on their own.

Without any explicit training or coaching from the researchers, the program became particularly good at recognizing human faces and body shapes—and cats, a mainstay of YouTube videos.

"We never told it during the training, this is a cat," Jeff Dean, the Google fellow who led the study, told the *New York Times*.[36] "It basically invented the concept of a cat."

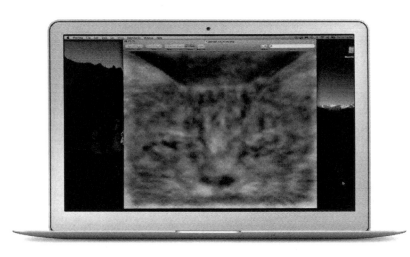

An image of a cat that a neural network taught itself to recognize. Credit Jim Wilson/The New York Times

The "Cat Paper" as it came to be known was a milestone in the field of AI, showing how the application of huge data sets to neural networks could generate never-seen-before accuracy in pattern recognition. The research will likely be seen decades hence as a watershed moment that advanced human understanding of how to use computers to structure, categorize, and make sense of incomprehensibly large amounts of raw, unstructured data.

HARDWARE ADVANCES HAVE MADE DEEP LEARNING ACCESSIBLE

The Cat Paper team benefited from the huge scale and resources of Google, building the largest neural network for machine learning ever seen at the time by connecting 16,000 computer processors. But since then, improvements to hardware have made it possible for any company to start applying Deep Learning algorithms to large data sets.

Engineers can now spin-up enormous, powerful servers and processors in a cloud architecture such as Amazon Web Services or Microsoft Azure using enormous data sets for pennies per processing cycle in a matter of hours. A huge advance also came in the repurposing of Graphic Processing Units (GPUs), which were developed primarily for the computer game industry. It turns out that, because of the huge data processing tasks that they are designed to be able to carry out in parallel, the latest GPUs are ideal for Deep Learning, typically reducing the time it takes to train a machine by an order of magnitude, thereby increasing the amount of data that can be tackled over a given period of time. As Nvidia, a leader in GPU manufacturing noted:

"Architecturally, the CPU is composed of just a few cores with lots of cache memory that can handle a few software threads at a time. In contrast, a GPU is composed of hundreds of cores that can handle thousands of threads simultaneously. The ability of a GPU with 100+ cores to process thousands of threads can accelerate some software by 100x over a CPU alone. What's more,

the GPU achieves this acceleration while being more power- and cost-efficient than a CPU."[37]

The Cat Paper research took three days to analyze 10 million images spread over 1,000 computers with 1 billion network connections. To get a sense of how fast computer power is advancing, just a year after running that original test Ng and researcher Adam Coates switched to GPUs using customized, off-the-shelf hardware widely available to prove that engineers can run a similar analysis involving 1 billion network connections using only 3 computers in a couple of days. If given 3 full days the team noted it can compute *11 billion* network connections. That was an order of magnitude improvement in computing power in just one year, using off-the-shelf technology.

> If given 3 full days the team noted it can compute *11 billion* network connections. That's an order of magnitude improvement in computing power in one year.

THE USE OF AI IN CUSTOMER SERVICE

While Natural Language Processing has been used for many years to provide sentiment analysis and trend insight, we're now starting to shift into an era when Deep Learning can be implemented to augment natural-language conversations without the frustration caused by the previous generation of chatbots.

With the shift in customer service interactions to digital channels, companies and platforms are now starting to build massive datasets of customer service conversations which can be used to train Deep Learning algorithms. Conversocial, for example, has a database of hundreds of millions of conversations that its clients have had with customers over social media and messaging platforms.

Messaging is particularly suited to Deep Learning because of the concise nature of the conversations happening between customers and brands. Unlike web chat, which is generally made up of many one-line interactions ("Hi," "I'm having a problem" etc.), Messaging, like SMS, generally is made up of complete questions and complete responses—a format that is much easier to use to train a Deep Learning system.

This is already starting to have an impact at some leading-edge companies who are already embracing the use of AI for customer service. The airline KLM gained a reputation as a pioneer in the social messaging space following their embracing of Twitter for customer service when the Icelandic volcano Eyjafjallajökull erupted in 2010, grounding thousands of flights in Europe. Since then their social care operation has grown, and they now receive over 100,000 mentions every week, with a team of 235 social care agents. To help them handle the volume, in 2016 they started piloting an AI-based system integrated into their customer care platform. Trained on an initial 60,000 questions and answers, the system suggests answers to the agents, who can adjust it if necessary before posting—and learns based on what the agents do. This enables them to handle more volume without losing the personal touch of agents:

"A personal approach is extremely important to KLM as this is what defines our social media service. Applying AI, KLM can handle a greater volume of questions while still maintaining its personal approach and speed."

—Tjalling Smit, Senior Vice President of Digital, KLM Royal Dutch Airlines[38]

In Part Two, we'll dig into how messaging and deep learning can be combined to create new forms of AI-augmented service with the potential to revolutionize service delivery and the customer experience.

KEY TAKEAWAYS

- Deep Learning techniques allow a computer system to learn complex representations within data, without any need for humans to categorize that data in advance.

- Neural Nets, the foundation of Deep Learning, can be used to create systems that have human-level accuracy in spotting patterns—but require large amounts of data to learn from, which was prohibitively slow and expensive in the past.

- In the last few years, advances in hardware have made it possible to apply Deep Learning techniques cheaply and efficiently to huge data sets, opening up Deep Learning techniques to be used in everyday use cases.

- With the shift into digital channels, and especially messaging, we're now entering a period where Deep Learning can be applied to customer service, with the potential to revolutionize service delivery.

PART TWO

Six Pillars for the Future of Customer Service

In a world where:

- Great service is all about speed and effort

- Any negative experience is one tweet away from going viral, and

- Every customer is mobile, and prefers to engage you in messaging channels

Companies need to rethink their approach to service. In Part Two, I outline the six key pillars of a customer service model that is designed for a world of instant answers, viral tweets, and integrated, intelligent systems. By adopting these pillars, companies can shift their service model away from having large numbers of relatively low-skilled agents mainly on the phone, to having a smaller number of highly skilled agents, supported and augmented by AI, delivering service over social messaging. The result will be a more effortless experience for customers (driving loyalty and repeat purchases), *and* reduced service costs.

The six pillars

Be Prepared for Crises
In the Social Era

Lean-in to The
Power of Messaging

Deploy Artificial
Intelligence Effectively

Make Effective Use of
Bot Technology

Use Social Agents as the
Model for Future Customer
Service Teams

Adopt a Messaging
Approach to all Digital
Channels

The six pillars

1. **Be prepared for crises in the Social Era.** We live in a world where social crises are now the new norm of doing business. Ensure that you are prepared to ride the storm and maintain customer sentiment when things go wrong.

2. **Lean-in to the power of messaging.** Messaging is a paradigm shift that fundamentally alters the ability of companies to deliver effortless and seamless service experiences. Learn how to manage messaging in the best way for service, and how to turn it into a primary service channel for your customers.

3. **Make effective use of bot technology.** New bot technology in Messenger and Twitter can backfire if you try to create standalone, rule-based chatbots that just get in the way. But used the right way, this functionality can simplify transactions for customers and act as a Visual IVR, increasing

the efficiency of your agents and speeding up resolution for customers.

4. **Deploy AI effectively.** Applying machine learning and AI to messaging-powered customer service has the potential to completely disrupt the customer service model. Take an iterative approach with a constantly improving system to gradually automate more and more, without negatively impacting the customer experience.

5. **Adopt a messaging approach to all digital channels.** The benefits of combining AI and human agents in the same conversation are enormous, but only possible in messaging. If you can't switch all of your service queries into social messaging channels, then instead shift your other digital channels into the asynchronous messaging paradigm.

6. **Use social agents as the model for future customer service teams.** Customer service teams of the future will be smaller, with most service volume coming through messaging channels, supported by automation and AI. With human agents reserved for escalation, they will need to be more highly trained and given more freedom than most agents today. This model closely resembles how social care teams are already operating.

CHAPTER 6

Be Prepared for Crises in the Social Era

● ●

In the 21st century, a social media savant can do more harm than a trial attorney.

—Jonathan Bernstein, Bernstein Crisis Management Inc.

On July 20, 2016 at 1pm, a router at Southwest Airlines' data center failed, causing a cascading technology crash that knocked reservation systems offline. A few tweets started coming into Southwest Airlines' social media team, with customers complaining that they couldn't check in for their flights or use the self-service kiosks at airports. That trickle of tweets rapidly turned into a deluge as the technical failure started grounding flights nationwide. The outage took four days to fully resolve, caused more than 2,300 flight cancellations and delays, and affected 250,000 passengers. In the confusion, travelers took to their phones and social channels to voice their frustration and try to figure out what was happening.

Southwest Airlines ✔
@SouthwestAir

A system outage has caused us to hold all departing flights. Flights in the air are not affected by this. All hands on deck to reslovle.

Ashley Cameron
@BohemianSolshyn

@SouthwestAir If flights in the air already weren't affected, why did my kid's flight have to land emergently in Kansas?!

A Southwest customer takes to Twitter during the outage.

The incident caused a massive spike in the volume of mentions Southwest received on Twitter, with almost 80,000 @mentions in the period July 20th–July 22nd—getting a month's worth of tweets in just three days. On July 21st, they received ~20x their normal daily Twitter volume (and this isn't even considering the amount of direct mentions they received, or posts and messages through Facebook and other social media channels).

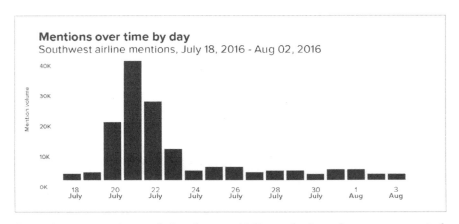

Incoming @mentions of Southwest Airlines during the outage period. Source: Brandwatch

Luckily, Southwest had a social media team that was ready to take rapid action. In an interview, Lisa Anderson (Southwest's Director of Social Business) said, "We had to react fast: using our listening system, we posted a pre-approved post on Twitter. We had to determine how we were going to handle this. We could not get information via email to our customer. All we knew was that our routers didn't work."[39]

Lisa noted that the team immediately went over the company's six communication principles before jumping into the social media storm:

1. Honest

2. Transparent

3. Quick

4. Genuine

5. Progressive

6. Omni-channel

The first thing they did was turn to Facebook Live, with their Chief Communication Officer expressing an apology over video that could go out to both media and individual customers at the same time, a great move that was much more impactful than just issuing a press announcement (that would have taken hours to trickle through to customers).

Southwest Airlines' Chief Communication Officer on Facebook Live shortly after the incident started affecting passengers.

The social care team then jumped into the fray, with all hands on deck to respond as quickly as possible to as many customers as possible. Because of this, they were able to minimize social blowback and even started to get positive feedback: "Suddenly, we started receiving positive posts. We had positive sentiment," said Ms. Anderson. That's a huge achievement in such a difficult situation.

SOCIAL CRISES ARE THE NEW NORMAL

A major gaming company we work with had four separate incidents in the summer of 2016 that caused spikes in mentions, averaging a 550% increase in inbound social volume over each incident compared to normal.

Every airline we work with regularly faces weather issues or flight cancellations that cause spikes in volume, and that's before technology failures and videos from customers who've been denied boarding somehow.

The same is true for telcos: when we analyzed the public inbound @ mentions of AT&T, Sprint, and T-Mobile in the US in the second half of 2016, we saw a pattern of semi-regular spikes causing huge increases in inbound volumes that their social care teams had to deal with.

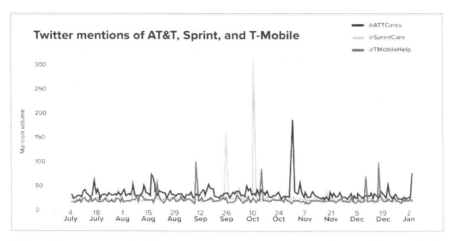

Network outages and other issues at AT&T, Sprint, and T-Mobile regularly cause major spikes in incoming volume over social. Source: Brandwatch

In this day and age, when something goes wrong everyone goes to social media first, both to complain and to find out what's happening. When one large cable company we work with experienced an outage during the night of a major sporting event, their incoming volumes in social increased by *1,900%*. When a major grocery chain came under fire for selling mislabeled meat, *98% of all related inbound queries the contact center received* came through social media.

In the social era, the traditional approach to major incidents—corporate silence or stone-faced PR statements—no longer meets the expectations of your customers. The social cycle happens at 10x the speed of the news cycle. By the time your official statement to the press has been published, you'll have already completely lost control of the message. The only way to prevent this is to move at the speed of social as well.

HOW YOUR SOCIAL CARE TEAM RESPONDS HAS A BIG IMPACT ON THE OUTCOME

If Southwest hadn't responded as quickly, transparently, and genuinely as they did, the outcome would have been much worse. They suffered a big loss from the grounded planes, but because of the way they communicated with their customers throughout the period—most of which was through social media—they created a lot of positive good will. This was true in the big ways (the Facebook Live video with their Chief Communication Officer), as well as the small ways—like saying sorry, genuinely.

Southwest Airlines
@SouthwestAir

@youloveit32 We're so sorry to hear about the cancellation and we cannot thank you enough for your patience with our services today. ^AC

The Southwest Airlines social care team apologizing over Twitter, in a good sign of being genuine despite a difficult situation.

In another airline incident in March 2017, United came under fire for turning away two young women at the gate for wearing leggings, considered "inappropriate clothing," when someone watching the incident tweeted about it. This blew up into a major issue that was covered by major publications, including the *New York Times*, who reported that "[Barring the girls] set off waves of anger on social media, with users criticizing what they called an intrusive, sexist policy, but the airline maintained its support for the gate agent's decision."[40]

Unfortunately, this issue could have been quickly turned into a nonissue if United had responded differently when it first arose. It turned out that the women were traveling on a free employee pass—and that United (like other airlines) requires employees and their family members to comply with a dress code when they are flying for free on behalf of the airline. Although some people may still have issue with this policy, it would have been a very different outrage compared to that caused when people falsely believed this to be a general dress policy for female travelers.

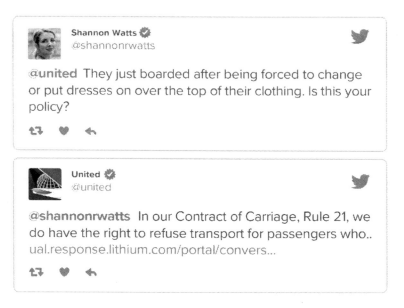

The first response from United, while technically correct, didn't correct the assumptions that this was a policy decision for normal travelers.

If United had moved quickly to say instead "Normal passengers can wear whatever they want! We only have a code for when people fly for free on employee passes, like these passengers" then the situation would have likely diffused before blowing up into a major incident. Indeed, hours later they did publish a message along these lines—unfortunately much of the damage had already been done by that point. This is an unfortunate example where no one did anything *wrong*—but responding differently (in a faster, more genuine and human way) would have had a much more positive impact.

United's full response, posted to social media later that day, which diffused the situation.

HAVE A CRISIS PLAN READY IN ADVANCE

To ensure you're not caught flatfooted, it's essential you have a clear process in place for what to do when a crisis hits. Given the market-impacting severity of any crisis that sweeps social media today, this means a response must be formulated at the corporate level.

The first thing to have a clear view of (at least, as much as is possible) is what exactly constitutes a crisis, or something with the potential to become a crisis. Pure numbers can be helpful here—for example, monitoring if any individual customer post mentioning your brand starts rapidly getting likes or retweets it's a sign that it needs careful assessing for risk. Similarly, it's essential to monitor overall volumes of messages and mentions you are receiving, benchmarked against the normal volumes you receive in any given hour or day.

Whenever the social care team spots something that could end up blowing up (and they'll often spot it first—issues will often hit social media sites before they are escalated through internal channels) they need to be able to rapidly escalate it up to corporate communications, and with both teams working hand-in-hand to formulate an approach in a very short time frame. Once the response is formulated, the social care team needs to then be able to have the freedom to get out there and get back to customers.

How do social agents know what to answer themselves and what to escalate? Have clear guidelines in place for what social agents can handle themselves, and what potential warning signs would require escalation (first up to a manager, then up to corporate comms). Your front-line agents should be equipped with a continually updated list of topics that will need comms approval when formulating a response.

Seven key principles to keep in mind when a crisis hits:

1. **Stop press**: When the crisis first hits, stop all comms leaving the building in order to evaluate, escalate and agree on your plan of attack. Keep this time period as short as possible.

2. **Communicate internally**: It's essential for everyone in the business to be on the same page, not just the social team. Every employee (including front-line staff) must clearly communicate the same message.

3. **Acknowledge and engage with confidence**: It's important to acknowledge the issue head on. If there is fault, even minor, it's essential to apologize and commit to fixing the issue in the future.

4. **Communicate compassion, concern, commitment, and control**: Your customers need to know that you care. Getting

out there quickly with compassionate responses is the best way to show this.

5. **Be open, honest, and human**: Even when a particular message needs to get out, this shouldn't look like corporate PR-speak. Give your agents clear information and guidance, but allow them to maintain personality and be themselves.

6. **You can't win them all over**: Every company is afflicted with trolls, and a crisis can bring a lot more out of the woodwork. If someone is just being aggressive and rude no matter what you say, then don't keep responding beyond getting your key messages across.

7. **The world hasn't ended:** Crises are tough, but it's important to keep your head, and make sure that you're not dropping the ball on other genuine customer service issues that are still happening.

"I tell my agents: if it makes you cringe, call me."

–Michael Roy, Social Care Program Lead, Alaska Airlines

BE READY TO SHIFT AGENTS OVER TO SOCIAL—QUICKLY

The potential for social media and messaging volumes to blow up unexpectedly whenever a crisis hits means that every company needs to be prepared to deal with significantly larger volumes than they are used to, at the drop of a hat. A crisis will get worse if you don't have the bandwidth to respond to your customers—but at the same time, you don't want a crisis situation to get worse because you have a load of untrained agents loose on social media without the right processes in place.

It's essential to have two key things in place:

1. A wider pool of agents trained in social media
2. A process for having non-social agents in the platform

Wider pool of agents trained in social media

This can be achieved by maintaining a "reserve pool" of agents whose normal job is in other channels (ideally other digital channels like chat or email, so they have strong writing skills), but who receive training in social media and your social media response processes, and who can be drawn on whenever volumes spike above the levels of the normal team. An alternative is to not have a dedicated social care team at all, but just to have social and messaging shifts among a wider pool of digital agents, all of whom are trained on social. In the latter model it can be hard to ensure all agents have the requisite skill level for normal social care, but if successful it gives you a very wide pool with current training and experience.

Process for having non-social agents in the platform

If a crisis situation requires you to pull in agents who aren't used to responding in social media, it's important to have a process for how this will work. For example—should these agents have full permissions, or should they be limited from doing certain actions (like deleting or liking posts)? Should they be able to respond to everything, or only private messages? If they are responding publicly, should these responses go through an approval workflow? Would a manager-approval workflow process be sufficient, or will you need to set up a peer-approval workflow process instead? Do your normal social agents know how to handle that if the situation arises?

It's essential that all of these steps are in place before your next crisis hits—which could be today.

PUBLISH UPDATES TO ENSURE YOU'RE REACHING AS MANY PEOPLE AS POSSIBLE

Social media crosses the line between 1:1 communication (especially over messaging) as well as 1:many. In a crisis, the ability to publish posts is a powerful way of getting the message out as quickly as possible to as many people as possible. It doesn't mean you can ignore people who've reached out 1:1—but having informative updates as the first thing that people see when they come to your social media properties will reduce the amount of inbound questions.

During the Southwest crisis, after the Facebook Live video was published they continued to follow up with additional posts, photos, and videos giving updates on the situation. "Words are great, but if you could do a quick photo that showed an airport and gave information, or if you put a person on Periscope or Facebook Live to give the update, the sentiment scores change quickly," said Southwest's Lisa Anderson at the time. "You can watch the sentiment move to neutral, or even into positive territory when the user can see somebody talking to them or see an image."

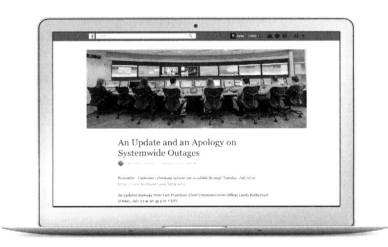

Southwest Airlines posting an update on the outage to their Facebook page.

An important parallel to this is that when a crisis hits, it's essential all marketing posts to social media properties stop immediately. There's nothing worse than blasting out a pre-scheduled flight promotion just as all your passengers have been grounded.

DON'T LOSE TRACK OF NORMAL SERVICE ISSUES IN THE NOISE

When a crisis hits, an understandable reaction can be to drop everything and focus 100% on just dealing with that particular crisis. But what if you are continuing to receive normal service requests over that period? If these get ignored, you'll have even more upset customers (and a big backlog to deal with once the crisis passes). Maintaining normal service levels during a crisis period is extremely difficult, but should be factored into your resourcing plans when bringing on additional heads. In order to do this, you need to ensure that your social care platform is set up to be able to filter messages relating to the crisis event into separate agent work queues than normal service issues, and that you are able to turn on this "crisis routing" as soon as an incident happens.

AI ISN'T MUCH HELP IN A NEW CRISIS

The unexpectedness with which most crises hit means that, unfortunately, it's very hard for AI or bots to offer much support. Unless you've experienced the same kind of crisis before, a Deep Learning system won't have been trained on how to respond, and it will be up to your human agents to take the slack.

Similarly, it's unlikely that you'll have time to create a Twitter or Messenger bot just to help with the crisis. However, if you face regular crises with similar types of issues (e.g., weather issues for airlines), it would be possible to create a bot designed to help with these situations which you can just turn on for relevant periods.

Using "Visual IVR" (described in Chapter 8) in private messaging can help with the volume, especially if you are able to quickly change this to include wording and routing particular to the crisis. To make the most of this, ensure you are telling customers to contact you privately over DM or Messenger in order to answer questions about the crisis—but, be ready for many customers to come to you publicly regardless.

KEY TAKEAWAYS

- Social crises are the new normal. Whenever something goes wrong (a technical outage, a weather issue, a negative service incident) everyone flocks to social media, both to complain and to get the latest updates.

- How your social care team responds has a big impact on the outcome. Respond quickly, honestly, and in a human way, and you will receive a positive response. If you go silent or respond only in corporate-speak you'll be punished for it.

- Have a crisis plan figured out in advance with your corporate communications team, with clear guidance on what kind of issues need escalation.

- Be ready to quickly shift additional agents into the social team when a crisis hits, with a process in place for how to manage a bigger team with varying levels of skills.

- Publish regular updates on the crisis to your social media properties, making use of video and photos where possible.

- Don't lose track of normal customer service issues during the crisis, and factor this into your resourcing requirements.

- AI and bots are unlikely to be able to help much, unless you've created a bot in advance to help with a crisis situation you know you face semi-regularly.

CHAPTER 7

Lean-in to the Power of Messaging

By 2019, we expect customer service inquiries received through consumer messaging apps alone will surpass such requests coming through social media. Make mobile messaging and, in particular, consumer messaging apps, a priority.

—Charles Golvin, Research Director, Gartner for Marketers[41]

Imagine this. You're on a work trip. Your flight was delayed, you're tired, and are walking through the airport, about to book an Uber to your hotel. You open the confirmation email to get the hotel address and see there's been a mess-up—you're booked to stay *tomorrow*, not *today*. Nightmare. You're going to have to phone them, wait on hold, repeat to the agent all of your booking details from the email while you're on the phone—all while trying to walk, flustered and tired, through the airport.

It would be different if you were a Hyatt Gold customer. On all of their contact pages—website, email, mobile app—there's a direct link to start a chat with their agents over Messenger (or Twitter DM). You can also just open Messenger and type in Hyatt. They've integrated Conversocial with their loyalty system, so as soon as you message them, they know exactly who you are, which hotel you're staying at, and all of your preferences. You can just send them a simple message saying that you've been booked to stay tomorrow instead of tonight. They don't need to ask you for any other details, and they'll get back to you in minutes. That's an incredible experience, and completely effortless. And it's possible because they've leaned in to the power of messaging.

SOCIAL MESSAGING IS A REVOLUTION IN SERVICE

Social messaging differs from traditional service channels because of its richer feature set—enabling brands to combine asynchronous messaging, live chat, interactive experiences, and automation in a single, continuous conversation that is always available to both brand and consumer at the tap of a button.

As a customer, the convenience of having a service conversation over messaging, in the same mobile app you're in with your friends, is huge. This ease of use is one of the biggest drivers of why consumers prefer messaging. In the Conversocial report *The State of Social Customer Service*, over half of respondents (54.4%) preferred new messaging channels as their primary form of brand communication over legacy channels such as email, phone, and web chat.

There are a few key factors that make messaging such a revolutionary channel for customer service:

1. Messaging combines real-time chat with asynchronous communication, giving customers and brands the best of both worlds: in-the-moment service, without requiring full attention at all times.

2. Messaging apps are platforms where interactive experiences, automated self-help, and transactions (e.g., making a reservation) can all be built and delivered to customers whenever they need it, without the need to download any other applications.

3. The messaging paradigm enables AI to work seamlessly alongside human agents in the same conversation, increasing the speed of response for consumers and making messaging more efficient to manage than any other service channel.

As Gartner for Marketers research director Charles Golvin noted, "Given its social nature, mobile messaging provides an opportunity to increase customer care efficiency, deflect phone calls to the less expensive messaging channel and grow customer satisfaction. Today, we estimate that 2% of all customer service inquiries are managed over mobile messaging. By 2019, we expect customer service inquiries received through consumer messaging apps alone will surpass such requests coming through social media. Make mobile messaging and, in particular, consumer messaging apps, a priority. This is even more critical for organizations that receive high volumes of social-media-based customer service requests."[42]

Asynchronicity is one of the key factors that makes social messaging apps like Messenger and WeChat so convenient and powerful. A consumer can start a conversation with a brand, do something else more important and then pick up the same conversation right where he left off 10 or 30 minutes later. Gone are the days of waiting on hold. Gone are the days of being 100% engaged in a webchat and nothing else. Now you can order a coffee, talk to a friend, and have your service issue resolved all at the same time.

In this chapter, I will focus on some of the key things you need to keep in mind in order to have human agents deliver an incredible, effortless service experience to your customers through messaging apps.

DELIVERING CUSTOMER SERVICE OVER MESSAGING

While the 1:1, private nature of messaging is in some ways very similar to live chat (as we'll get into later), there are a few key ways it is different—and this has an impact on workflow, KPIs, and agent training:

- The asynchronous nature means that conversations can pause and resume between messages. Agents need to be able to have a real-time conversation while the customer is present, but be able to seamlessly shift to the next conversation if they are waiting on the customer.

- Waiting on the customer can sometimes take days. This means the agent picking up that conversation needs to be able to quickly read up on the background of the conversation and continue where it was left off.

- Although some messaging apps are standalone (e.g., WhatsApp), some are closely intertwined with a public social presence (e.g., Facebook and Twitter). In those cases, conversations can switch between public and private posts—so agents need to be able to track conversations as they switch, and understand how to respond differently in the public vs. private spheres.

Whereas the first two can be mostly solved with technology, the third requires workforce decisions and training. Generally, there are two models:

Split social & messaging teams

In this case, you have a specific team of agents trained how to respond publicly, and who handle all public responses from the brand handle. When they refer a conversation to private messaging, it is also handed off to a separate team of agents (who must be able to see the full history of the public conversation, to avoid repeating any questions). There can then be a wider pool of agents who only handle private messaging, which (because it's exclusively private) makes it easier to pull these agents from a wider digital service team. This model is more likely to be seen in companies with very large volumes and hundreds of agents.

Combined social & messaging team

In this case, there is a single team of agents who are fully trained on both social media and messaging, and who own a conversation through both public and private elements of the conversation. In this case, all of the agents are likely to be dedicated to social and messaging instead of coming from a wider digital agent pool. This is simpler from a workflow perspective, and is more common in companies with lower volumes and less than 100 agents handling social and messaging volumes.

MEASURING "CASES" IN THE MESSAGING PARADIGM

When Frankie Saucier was in charge of digital customer care channels for Cox Communications, the third largest telco in the US, she knew her service metrics inside and out. Her role encompassed social care, web chat (for support) and email, and she had to make the case for why the company should allocate investment in digital and social care every year to company executives.

With call centers, email, and chat it was straightforward: calculate your cost per issue by analyzing the volume of calls, email cases, and chat sessions against the volume and cost of the labor needed to staff those calls, emails, and chats. But when she got to social and messaging, Frankie noticed that the company was missing the analysis needed to make an apples-to-apples business case to determine the ROI of investing in social channels versus other channels.

Over the phone or in a live chat there's a clear beginning and end of every conversation, which makes them relatively simple in terms of case management, routing, and tracking. It's easy to calculate important metrics like average handling time and cost-per-resolution in a simple, consistent way. But when you deliver service over continuous, people-based conversations it becomes much harder to define an issue in the same way. If someone responds in the same thread, the day after you thought the issue was closed, is this a new issue? Or was your definition of closed wrong, and needs correcting? If someone messages you a compliment, then an hour later asks a service question, when does the case start?

These difficulties have made many in the industry try to claim that social and messaging are just different, and require different metrics. But this lack of comparable metrics is a major issue that has held back many companies from making the necessary investments into messaging as a service channel. When major analyst firms such as McKinsey, Nielsen and Gartner say that the average cost-per-resolution in social and messaging is much lower than email and phone,[43] it persuades early adopters and innovators to jump in. But more mainstream and pragmatic companies want to see this in their own data before they invest in a significant way.

This is exactly what Frankie found when she rolled up her sleeves and dug into the data. When she peeled back the layers of social messaging, with its asynchronous nature, she came to a startling insight: most of her industry was artificially depressing the potential volume going into social and messaging, because they didn't truly realize that the cost is actually a lot lower than phone and even chat. It was just that nobody knew how many real issues were being resolved by social agents.

The secret to making this calculation lies in clarifying how many customer service interactions it takes to complete a customer event so it can be equated to a phone call. As Frankie said, "How many of these social care interactions equal one hello-to-goodbye phone call?"

"Many companies will tell you that, percentage-wise, 85% of their interactions with customers are still happening over the telephone, and only 1% of their transactions are happening on social media. The reason for that is

because they can't see a solid business reason to grow social media customer care because getting to that data is either too hard, or they can't match it apples to apples."

—Frankie Saucier

This is where technology must come in. Just as you will fail if you try to treat messaging like it's a normal service channel (putting it into the same workflow as web chat, for example), you will also fail if you try and treat it as a completely separate beast that can only stand on its own. Instead, intelligent design decisions must be made in your customer care platforms to ensure that you account for the unique elements of managing a conversation over messaging, while still creating fixed data points for case opening and closing that allow you to make direct comparisons with phone and chat. You need to have processes—both manual and automatic—to close a conversation, either when an agent judges it to have been resolved, or if the customer doesn't follow up after a certain amount of time. This ticket close needs to be permanent to ensure a clean data set that is comparable to the phone channel, and to prevent your historical data changing day to day (for example having an old case be reopened by a new message). However, you also need to account for the continuous nature of messaging, for example enabling agents to have later follow ups that don't count toward the case close time, and mechanisms to deal with additional messages that come in after closing the case but don't require opening a full new case (for example, the customer saying thank you).

PROMOTING MESSAGING TO YOUR CUSTOMERS

Most companies didn't ask their customers to start complaining over social media. Customers realized that it was a powerful channel to get attention and get issues resolved when they weren't getting the level of service they expected from other channels. From there it continued to grow. But there's a limit to this natural growth. Social will always be there as an escalation channel, but to turn private, 1:1 messaging into a primary service channel requires that your customers know:

- That they can contact you on messaging for a serious service issue

- That it will be resolved fully within messaging (they won't be required to phone or email after reaching out)

- That they'll get a response in minutes, not hours

Without customers being aware of these elements, they are more likely to phone with an urgent or serious issue—costing more money to resolve, and taking more effort by the customer (decreasing their NPS). Whereas the last two are brand promises that you can signal in messaging (but need to consistently deliver in practice), the first is about active promotion of messaging buttons across customer touch-points.

There are a number of different ways you can promote messaging:

1. Add "Message us" and "DM us" buttons to the contact pages of your website and mobile app

2. Promote social and messaging channels offline

3. Use Facebook and Twitter business functionality to be clear you provide support and respond to messages

4. Route from other service channels

1. *"Message us" and "DM us" buttons on your website and mobile app*

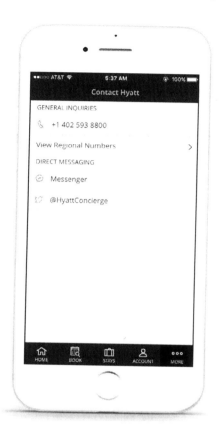

Hyatt promoting Messenger and Twitter on the contact page of their mobile application.

Message us button on Hyatt hotel property websites.

2. Offline promotion of social and messaging channels

Delta promoting Twitter customer service in their in-flight magazine.

Facebook Messenger allows you to create a unique QR code for your business that you can promote offline. Taking a photo of the image using your Messenger camera will start a chat with your agents.

3. Use Facebook and Twitter business functionality to be clear you provide support and respond to messages

On Facebook, you can opt to display how quickly your brand responds to messages.

Twitter now enables you to define a business account as "providing support," which is shown when a customer searches for your handle.

4. Route from other service channels

The final method has the potential to have the most impact on deflection. This is to actively encourage customers to turn to messaging when they phone or email—for example, telling them they can wait 40 minutes on hold, or start a Messenger chat with an agent right now. A simple way to do this is to simply share your Twitter or Messenger handle, so the customer can initiate the conversation. A more complex but powerful way is to proactively initiate the messaging chat—for example by using Messenger APIs to look up the customers phone number, and see if there's a match on Messenger (this API is only available by request from Facebook).

HOW QUICKLY DO YOU NEED TO RESPOND?

"Speed is part of the Twitter promise. Twitter is about what's happening now, so if I engage on Twitter there's an expectation that I'm going to get a faster response. There's data that shows that people prefer the service experience on Twitter than in person. You think, "How could it be even better to have an experience via Tweet than talking to a human in person and getting help?" The answer is speed."

—Chris Moody, GM Data & Enterprise Solutions at Twitter

Messaging sits at the intersection of real-time, in-the-moment chat and asynchronous conversations that can be responded to at any time in the future. Although it may be convenient to think of messaging more like email (that can have a response time in hours or days) this would be a huge mistake. Messaging has the potential to replace phone calls—but only if customers know they will get a quick response. Although this doesn't have to be in seconds like in web chat, the goal should be to respond in minutes—then to keep the conversation close to real time while the customer is present and typing. It's *the customer* who can choose to leave the conversation and come back tomorrow—not your agents.

It's *the customer* who can choose to leave the conversation and come back tomorrow—not your agents.

The goal should be to make resolving a service issue as fast and effortless as messaging a friend to organize lunch.

To deliver this level of service, you need to resource your social and messaging team in the same way you resource chat—carefully tracking utilization over the course of a day, and ensuring you have enough agents to always have a very small amount of slack.

The only time an agent should be coming back days later is when they are checking up on an unresolved issue (e.g., to see if a replacement part was delivered and installed OK). In this situation, agents can make use of the continuous nature of messaging conversations (and notifications) to ensure no case gets left unresolved.

CUSTOMER DATA, SECURITY, AND AUTHENTICATION

IT and Security teams are used to requiring vendors who hold customer information to sign contracts that guarantee they will follow certain security protocols, and that insure them against data loss or leaks. But they can't get those same agreements from Facebook or Twitter. This fact, combined with the relative newness of the channels, make many companies wary of taking any customer information over even private messaging.

This is, however, a mistake.

It's been widely accepted for decades that "First Contact Resolution" is one of the key requirements to delivering a positive service experience. This was backed up in the research CEB conducted for *Effortless Experience*:

requiring customers to switch channels and repeat information is a major driver of frustration and disloyalty.

So how do you solve this challenge?

The first step is to educate IT and Security teams on how social media and mobile messaging platforms work. The security of private messaging through Messenger or Twitter is similar to—if not stronger than—email. If your customer service team is authorized to ask for certain information over email, then you should get the same authorizations for private messaging.

However, for some companies even email is not considered a secure enough channel for customer information—especially in regulated industries such as telco, healthcare, or finance. In this situation, it's essential to create a secure method to authenticate customer identity and take personal information without that data passing through the messaging platforms.

Both Twitter and Messenger allow you to open a secure web view from within the messaging thread. In this webview, either IT teams or external vendors like Conversocial can build a secure site to take personal information and authenticate the customer's identity. After this process is complete, the customer can seamlessly return to the messaging thread to finish the conversation and resolve the issue. They haven't had to leave the messaging app, but have been able to share their personal information in a completely secure way. This kind of authentication mechanism takes some work (from both your internal IT teams and external vendors), but the result—being able to fully resolve any issue inside messaging—is more than worth it.

ACHIEVING A SINGLE VIEW OF THE CUSTOMER

One of the most powerful elements of delivering service over messaging is that you have a continuous conversation with the same customer for all time—so you can gather lots of information about who they are that is always visible to agents, whenever they reach out.

This power is magnified 10x when you combine social and messaging identity with your own customer data.

There are a number of different types of integrations that you can do—which combination is right for you depends on the systems you have in place, and the types of issues you are handling.

CRM Integration

As in the Hyatt example at the beginning of the chapter, by integrating loyalty or CRM systems with your customer care platform it becomes possible for agents to create matches between the data sets. This means whenever a customer messages a brand, the agent can see any relevant customer information (such as which hotel they are staying at, or which flight they're about to take), enabling them to resolve issues completely effortlessly. The match between customers can be stored either in the customer care platform or within the CRM (if it has fields for social/messaging IDs).

Case History

Until you've managed to move 100% of your service interactions to messaging, it's likely that customers will still occasionally be phoning you. In this situation, it's essential that your phone agents can see the history in social and messaging, and vice versa. Sharing this information can either be done via central notes in the CRM, or by direct integration between different systems.

Social Login

The simplest way of matching identity between CRM identifiers (such as an email address) and social or messaging IDs is to have an agent ask for this information in the messaging thread, then save that connection. However, it's even more effortless if this match can be done before a customer ever reaches out. The easiest way to do this is to collect social and messaging IDs within the normal customer journey, for example by using social log-in tools on your website or app.

Integrated Messenger Receipts

An option unique to Facebook Messenger is to integrate transaction receipts directly into your order flow. This initiates the Messenger thread with the customer as soon as they've made a purchase, so it's easy for them to find if they have a question. And when they do reach out, the order history is right there for the agent to see.

Integrated Messenger receipts on the Everlane ecommerce website.

KEY TAKEAWAYS

- The defining characteristic of messaging is its combination of real-time and asynchronous messages. This means that agents need to be able to have a real-time conversation while the customer is present, but to seamlessly shift to the next conversation if they're waiting on the customer.

- Defining a "case" in the messaging paradigm is much more difficult than on phone and email—but it's essential to have comparable metrics on handling time and cost-per-resolution in order to build a business case to invest in messaging.

- To make messaging a primary service channel (and to deflect phone calls), you must promote it to your customers (both online and offline). Customers need to know that if they reach out, they will get a response in minutes and be able to fully resolve their issue without being deflected to other channels.

- As a rule of thumb, you should treat private messaging the same way you treat email for consideration of what customer data it's OK to ask for. For additional security, take information over secure webviews opened inside the messaging threads.

- Integrate messaging IDs with your own customer record to create a completely effortless service experience for both consumers and agents.

CHAPTER 8

Make Effective Use of Bot Technology

● ●

People don't need another app, they need a better way to connect with businesses. Build meaningful relationships through messaging.

—Shane Mac, CEO and Founder of Assist

"Hi, I'm looking for some help. I made an order three weeks ago, but I've just opened it, and I want to return it. Is that OK?"

"You'd like to make an order? That's great! What color are you looking for?"

"What? I'm sorry, I'm trying to RETURN an order. Are you a bot? Can I speak to a human?"

"I'm sorry, I don't understand what color you are looking for. The options are black, red, blue, orange or grey. Please select one of the available colors."

"TAKE ME TO A HUMAN"

"I'm sorry, that's not a color we have available."

Unfortunately, this is the kind of experience that too many customers have had with bots. After the launch of the bot platforms in 2016, companies rushed to build interactive bots, usually focused on ordering or other commerce use cases. Unfortunately, many of these were poorly designed, rule-based bots with weak natural language processing (NLP) or understanding of intent—and many were launched without the knowledge of the customer care department, and without any thought as to how service issues would be handed from bot to human agents.

AVOIDING CHAT BOT 2.0

Chatbots aren't new. In previous decades, many companies tried to implement bots within their web chat environments. The results were, for the most part, disastrous—with an experience similar to the one described earlier. Rule-based bots with NLP aren't smart enough to handle general free-flowing conversations; and the hand-off to a human agent can be a frustrating experience, especially in a web chat environment. Considering that human-powered chat is cheaper to provide than a phone call, why build an automated chat experience that frustrates the customer, and leads them to phone anyway?

The mistake that many companies made with the launch of the messaging app bot platforms was to try and replicate this same experience. However, messaging is different from web chat in many ways, and these differences mean that bots and automated functionality *can* add a huge amount of value—if they're done in the right way.

VISUAL IVR

The easiest way for bot functionality to add instant value is to use it as a method for "Visual IVR." In any service conversation, the first few messages are generally used to identify the type of issue the customer is facing, and then to collect relevant information needed to resolve the issue. Generally, this routing and data collection is incredibly simple to automate, without needing to make use of any natural language processing that could go wrong.

Both Messenger and Twitter enable you to have automated welcome messages with button navigation options (instead of a keyboard). This functionality can be used to discover what kind of issue the customer has, then ask them for relevant information—and only then take them to an agent. This kind of Visual IVR system can immediately save 15–20% of messaging volumes—a huge saving in agent time—while improving routing accuracy, and accelerating resolution time for the customer.

An example of Visual IVR when you DM Abercrombie & Fitch on Twitter. After providing your order number, you get taken to an agent seamlessly.

SMART INTEGRATIONS FOR SELF-SERVE RESOLUTION

Depending on what type of service you provide, there are often some common requests that would be easy for customers to resolve seamlessly with a self-service option. For example, airline customer service teams often get asked about the status of a flight. Ecommerce retailers get asked when an order is due to be delivered. Grocery chains get asked where the nearest store is. Most of these questions can be answered by taking a single, specific piece of data (flight number, order reference, zip code etc.) and doing a look up in the relevant internal system.

Again, this kind of integration doesn't require any natural language processing or intelligence in conversation flow. It can be done with menu buttons and simple data entry, which simplifies the implementation significantly and reduces the chance of creating a frustrating experience for your customers. But the benefits are enormous—your customers get their answer instantly and effortlessly, and your agents are spared from repetitive tasks.

United Airlines has an automated flight-status checker within Twitter DMs. If you don't use their mobile app, then this is much faster than asking a human agent or looking it up on the mobile web.

TRANSACTIONAL BOTS

The next level up is to build more fully featured bots for more complex transactions such as ordering flowers, booking a hotel room, or making an appointment. Doing this correctly requires more than just menu buttons, and needs to include conversational free text elements that can be understood by the bot. This is easy to get wrong—and if you have a strict decision tree, it's easy for a customer to get frustrated.

This doesn't mean that bots are a bad idea—it just means that they have to be smart enough to adapt to how the customer is choosing to make an order, including the ability for a customer to change their mind at any time. Bot developer Assist call this "Random Access Navigation"—the ability to collect the relevant intents in a free-flowing conversation, in any order, and allow any of them to be changed independently without having to restart the process.

If you decide to build a bot for complex transactions like this, it's important that you work with a specialized bot builder who has deep expertise in messaging and natural language processing, and who will build a bot that is flexible enough to take orders in a "natural" way. It's also essential to design the bot with the handoff to human agents in mind from day one.

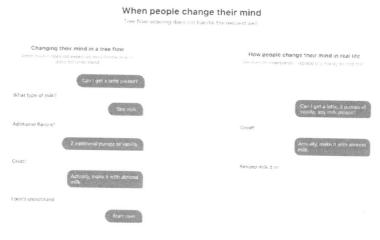

Source: Shane Mac / Assist

CASE STUDY: BUILDING A BETTER BOT WITH THE SEPHORA RESERVATIONS BOT

Shane Mac, CEO of bot developer Assist, describes how Sephora uses Messenger to reduce friction and improve the customer experience:

Sephora's a great example of a singular focus on automating a transactional exchange or specific, critical task for a brand. Sephora's goal is to get customers into a store. They do that with custom makeovers, personal one-on-ones, etc. You can get a facial and your makeup training at a store. It's a big initiative, but until the launch of their bot you had to call a phone number to book an appointment, or use a pop-up module on their website that takes around 20 steps to complete. You click on the item, pick your store, and it takes you through a whole tree flow.

We took that workflow and said, 'Let's just do reservations. Let's make it so in one step if a customer said *Can I get a makeover on Saturday at 9 a.m.* we'd be able to recognize and execute it.' If we have enough information, we can actually get this done in one step without a sign-up, without having to log in, without having to go to a website—all just by messaging Sephora.

We're building something called Random Acts of Navigation (RAN) which we think is a big shift in how you think about the experience. It allows customers to change their mind, which isn't possible in a normal bot decision tree. If you're talking to a Sephora agent on the phone and said, '*I want to do a makeover at 11am. Actually, can I do 1 p.m.?*' the change works because you're talking to a human. RAN allows customers to do that with a bot.

We train the Natural Language Processing (NLP) and machine learning algorithm to understand store name, store similarities, and even shorthand versions of names so that it still understands the intent. There are four 'intents' and four different scenarios in which the bot will respond based on what other data it has. This informs the way we write copy. If the bot already has the appointment time and the city but doesn't know the store name, then you have to write copy that says, 'When you have store name, and these two other intents, but missing this other one, what do you want the sentence to say?' Then you write four sentences for each step that could show up based on what data you do or do not have. You end up writing 16 queries. The consumer can now navigate this in any way she wants. She can go step by step like a tree flow or she can say *But I actually want to go to Powell Street. Can I do 11 a.m. tomorrow? Do you have something next Monday? Hold on, hold on. I want my makeup done, not a personal one-on-one.*

Today, everyone's writing a script. Two things happen when you write a script. First it tells the customer what they should do, not what the customer wants to do. The script has already failed. Second is that a customer can't really change her mind midway through and the whole process goes sideways. For a brand, pre-writing 10,000 queries that are all tied together with if/then statements everywhere is a disaster. It takes forever and then you're basically creating an entire experience that no consumer wants. The problem is then brands conclude that bots are really dumb.

The way that we think about it is to start with what the customer wants to do, then figure out the different intents needed to get there. With Sephora, it's book a reservation at a store. The intents we need for that are appointment time, type of appointment, name of the store, and the city it's in. The Sephora automated messenger experience is already converting 5% better than their mobile website converts, and now they're going to start driving traffic there. The phone number in the stores will now be 'Just message us instead.' That's a good example of real friction being reduced and we only did one thing—booking reservations.

Booking in a web view in 9 steps
It takes 9 steps to book a class on the Sephora website

Booking in 1 step with NLP
Leveraging natural language processing to identify all parameters

Booking with web views can be costly.
Forms with "next" button take time and learnability is low. Each form is different.

It's faster and easier to book an appointment using Sephora's Messenger bot than doing the same on their mobile website. Source: Shane Mac/Assist

ENSURING A SMOOTH HANDOFF BETWEEN BOTS AND HUMANS

Building out more fully featured bots (like Sephora's) is a great way to automate a transaction that otherwise may have had to take place in the mobile web or a native app—or over the phone. However, these only cover narrow use cases, and a customer will still need to speak to an agent if they have any question outside of the bot flow. If this handoff isn't handled well, it can be an incredibly frustrating experience for the customer.

Typical issues with bot > human hand-off include:

- Not having a simple, persistent menu button to get to an agent—requiring the customer to know and type in the correct query to get moved to an agent

- The bot still "listening" to the conversation after it's gone to a human agent, and then jumping in and responding automatically while the agent is trying to help

- The agent not having the full context of the bot conversation, so asking the customer to repeat what they'd already asked for

Fixing these issues is primarily a technical challenge that needs to be solved by both your bot and customer care platform—but are essential if a bot is to reduce effort for your customers, instead of just frustrating them. The best practice to handle this today is to have different messaging accounts for bots and human agents, with the handover handled by sharing a deep link to the customer that takes them straight into the relevant messaging thread (for example, the bot shares a link that takes the customer into the messenger thread for human agents). This is relatively seamless for customers, although does require your customer service platform to be able to listen to the bot conversations and display them as part of the conversation history when a customer is handed over. Although this isn't as seamless as having a single conversation thread, by having two separate conversations you avoid the risk of both bot and agent responding to the same message.

The good news is that both Facebook Messenger and Twitter have announced they are developing functionality that will allow the handoff between bots and humans to be managed programmatically by their APIs. This means that, as long as the bot and customer care platforms use those APIs, they can exist within the same messaging thread without any risk of missing a customer who needs help or of double-responding to the same message. This will be a huge step forward in enabling bots and human agents to exist seamlessly side by side.

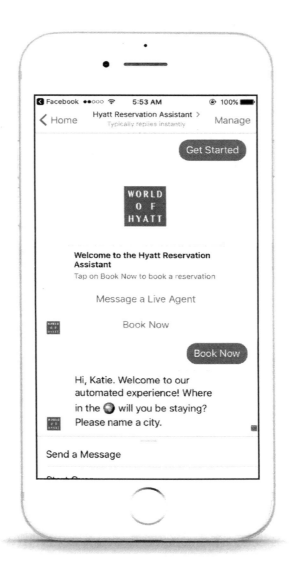

The Hyatt reservations bot on Messenger. When you first enter the messaging thread, you have the option of messaging a live agent—and this option remains in the menu at the bottom throughout the bot experience, making it easy to get to an agent whenever you need. Hyatt agents are able to view the history of the bot conversation, so there's no need to repeat any information.

KEY TAKEAWAYS

- Don't rush to build a complex automated bot, or you're at risk of making the same mistakes that were made in previous generations of chatbots—and will end up creating a frustrating experience that will lead to *more* phone calls, not less.

- Use automated bot functionality to build a Visual IVR that will route questions and collect information before getting to an agent, improving resolution speed and agent efficiency.

- Build smart integrations that allow customers to self-serve on common questions such as flight or order status.

- When considering more complex bots, choose a narrow focus area that will enable customers to get what they want in a faster and easier way than by using a mobile website or downloading a native application.

- Ensure bots are designed to allow customers to input data naturally and to make mistakes without starting again, and that the handoff between bot and human agent is seamless.

CHAPTER 9

Deploy Artificial Intelligence Effectively

• •

Who cares whether it's human-operated or not behind the scenes, the question is what can this thing do for me?

—Mike Schroepfer, Facebook CTO

In 2013, the same year that Facebook hit over 1 billion global users, Facebook CTO Mike Schroepfer set his sights on a hugely ambitious goal: to develop an AI assistant so powerful it could outperform a human. Through Facebook AI Research (FAIR), Schroepfer hired some of the best minds in AI in order to conduct research into Deep Learning and how to massively improve natural language understanding. What came out of it was a new AI assistant, called "M," that made use of Facebook Messenger to combine humans and AI behind the scenes in a way that is only possible in the messaging paradigm.

The human and AI combo enabled M to complete complicated, multi-step tasks. For example, M could not only purchase a gift for a friend online, it could also suggest what the gift should be and know which address it should be delivered to. Facebook M's human trainers, who supervised the answers being suggested by the AI system and handled anything that couldn't be automated, had customer service backgrounds. Over time, the AI system would learn from them to do more and more by itself.

Facebook is now implementing the M technology inside Messenger conversations for all of us (so, for example, when you suggest going to a restaurant to a friend in Messenger, M will pop up and ask if you'd like to make a reservation at that restaurant for the time you suggested). But the techniques behind M aren't unique to Facebook—they pave the way for how every other company can start applying AI into messaging conversations today.

HUMANITY AT SCALE, POWERED BY AI

The future of service will be less jarring than it is today in terms of how machines and human agents work together to solve an issue. Gone will be the days of a bot repeating "Sorry, I don't understand," only to have an agent come online and start the process from the beginning. Human agents and machines will work seamlessly to resolve an issue. Inside a single messaging conversation, you will see:

- Fully automated responses to simple questions, gathering information, or looking up data

- A combined human/AI response, where the AI suggests a potential response to a human agent to edit and approve

- Human agents responding to complex or emotional questions (supported in their own workflow by machine learning and automation in various ways)

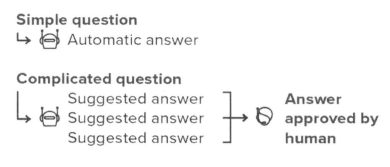

Simple question
↳ 🔊 Automatic answer

Complicated question
↳ 🔊 Suggested answer ⎤
       Suggested answer ⎬→ 🔊 **Answer approved by human**
       Suggested answer ⎦

Emotional/upset comment
↳ 🔊 Answer written by human

The different types of ways human agents and AI will combine to respond in messaging conversations.

This combination of human and machine will transform the customer service model, shifting us from a world where a large number of relatively low-skilled customer service agents handle the majority of service issues over the phone to a world where a smaller number of high-skilled agents handle the majority of service issues over digital messaging, supported by AI.

This is only possible because of the asynchronous nature of messaging.

WHY MESSAGING IS UNIQUELY SUITED TO AI

Over the phone or in a live chat environment, you can engage with an automated experience OR you can speak to a human. But it's impossible to combine them in a seamless way. Conversations that begin with automation invariably end up struggling to understand or not being able to help in some way, at which point the customer is frustrated and has to be handed off to a human agent—who often won't have the context of the conversation with the bot. What a terrible experience. For this reason, automation and chatbots have always been limited in usage in the customer service world. Despite being desperate to reduce service costs, chatbots were never the answer.

But messaging is different. The asynchronous nature means that it's completely fine to have a wait of minutes (or longer) between question and answer—unlike phone or chat, where this would kill the conversation. This wait means that humans and automation can sit side by side in a way that's never been possible before.

This model is similar to the Visual IVR in use by many brands today, described in the last chapter. When you send a DM to certain Twitter brand handles, an automated message begins triaging your request. Then, depending on the type of issue you select from a menu (such as returning an item) the Visual IVR functionality will automatically ask you for the relevant information needed to solve the issue. Once that information has been sent, a human agent will respond.

But whereas Visual IVR makes use of the bot functionality available in messaging to automate a certain number of predefined questions and messages, adding AI means using Deep Learning (and other advanced machine learning techniques) to train a system on a database of customer questions and agent responses in order to automate a much larger percentage of queries. This enables the development of a system that can automatically respond to unstructured, free text questions it may not have seen in that exact way before; a system that is constantly being trained by agents to be more accurate and to be able to answer more questions confidently. A system like this, for example, would be able to learn from historical conversations how to respond to all the different types of situations when someone may ask for a refund—without needing to have those rules written programmatically in advance.

A customer service system that combines all of these elements will be able to automate a constantly increasing percentage of service inquiries, without ever risking the customer experience. Answers will only be fully automated when the AI system is completely confident the answer is right;

in all other cases, the answer will either be human approved or human written. In turn, this will enable a smaller and smaller pool of agents to service customers in an increasingly faster and more effortless way. It will revolutionize the customer service model. This revolution is in its infancy right now—but all the relevant elements are in place to make it take off.

THE BENEFITS OF MESSAGING DATA

Machine learning relies on having large amounts of data to train a system on. Without large, relatively clean datasets, it's hard to fully utilize Deep Learning techniques. In this, messaging has two big advantages over other customer service channels:

Messaging conversations are concise

Whereas the fully live nature of web chat can have a tendency to break apart questions into multiple lines and responses, email has the opposite problem, with a much longer form factor that can include multiple different questions and statements in a single email. Both of these characteristics can make the data harder to analyze in a Deep Learning system. Although messaging isn't completely free of either of these afflictions, the norm in the messaging environment is to send complete questions and answers in each message, without any fluff on either side. This can make it much easier to use messaging data to train a Deep Learning system than more unstructured conversation formats.

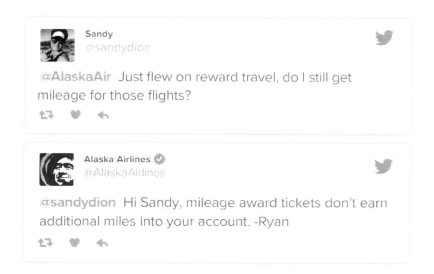

Example of the kind of complete questions and answers that are easy to train a Deep Learning system on.

Although this makes simple queries easy to automate, issues which require multiple messages back-and-forth are more complex. In these situations, automation may be able to handle the first message or two before being handed over to a human agent. These more complex interactions can still be automated over time, but will require larger data sets, and more careful guidance to get right.

Historical messaging data can be available through the platforms

Whereas switching to a new chat vendor could mean losing easy access to historical conversations (or having a copy in a data format that's hard to use for anything other than an archive), the main messaging platforms (Facebook Messenger, Twitter DMs etc.) maintain a full historical data set. Although these aren't open to everyone, some vendors who have partnerships with the platforms can access them (including Conversocial). This allows these vendors to have a historical dataset to train their systems on from day one, creating a major advantage (and this is before thinking about the data already collected by many vendors—Conversocial, for example, has a database of hundreds of millions of conversations).

TAKE AN ITERATIVE APPROACH

The best thing about a combined human and AI system in messaging is that you don't need to create an incredibly smart, comprehensive system that can respond to any open query from day one. By having a system that always has a human agent as a backstop, automation can step in only when it's confident. Customers never have a frustrating experience, and the automation can gradually get better and better over time. Our recommendation is to start with suggested responses, so that every response is being approved by a human agent. Then introduce fully automated responses as quality and confidence increases, with the AI handling a gradually increasing percentage of responses by itself.

SUGGESTED RESPONSES

The first place to start with Deep Learning is to have a system that suggests responses to a human agent in order to either approve them, edit them, or reject them. In this situation, when a question comes in that the automated system recognizes it will present what it thinks are potential correct answers, usually with a confidence rating by each one (this could be a single potential answer, or multiple potential answers). If the answer is correct, the agent just approves it and moves on to the next question, saving a huge amount of time. In this case, the system will have its response reinforced, training it that the answer was correct, and increasing its confidence level next time. If it's almost correct, then the agent can edit the response before posting, in doing so training the system with the edited answer. And if it's not correct at all, or doesn't have an answer, then the agent will just respond as normal (training the system with this new answer).

This system increases agent efficiency by making simple, repetitive answers a one-click process; and uses the agents' own corrections and responses to constantly train and improve the automated system.

AUTOMATED RESPONSES

With very common questions, the automated system will have a high confidence level that it knows the answer. In these situations, you can start to allow the system to respond automatically whenever it has a confidence above a certain percentage (e.g., 95%). Where you should set this cut off depends on a number of factors, including your confidence in the system after seeing how accurate it is with suggested responses.

The initial percentage of queries that can be automatically responded to from day one will depend on the variety and complexity of the queries your customer service team receives, as well as the amount of training data available. Anecdotal data from numerous large, consumer facing companies suggests that ~20% of queries can be fully automated after a short period of time, increasing to 30–40% after a period of reinforcement training by agents.

GOING BEYOND SIMPLE Q&A: HOW FACEBOOK USES "MEMNETS"

Although a Deep Learning system trained on customer service conversation data can become very effective at answering frequently asked questions and handling the first response to a query, additional work is needed to create a system that can handle multistep questions. This is needed in order to automate a higher percentage of customer service queries. The key to fixing this problem is in adding short term memory to Deep Learning, a technique that was used by DeepMind for AlphaGo and is now becoming more prevalent in advanced Deep Learning systems.

Facebook AI Research created a system to enable this that they call Memory Networks, or MemNets, which gives "short-term memory" to their Deep Learning systems, and enables those systems to reason from the input data. Facebook CTO Mike Schroepfer explains:

"One of the challenges with AI systems is many of the existing systems are dumb pattern matchers; you ask it a question, it gives you an answer, it doesn't learn as it goes. So one of the challenges with Memory Networks is can we take a neural net, this thing that you train, and can we attach a short-term memory to it so that it can take in data and answer questions based on that data."[44]

For example, when they deployed the MemNets system into M, it automatically learned how to handle the first couple of questions when someone asked for help ordering flowers: "What's your budget?" and "Where are you sending them?"[45] In effect, this enables AI systems to apply logic and reasoning to memories—a more human way of thinking.

USE AI BEHIND THE SCENES TO INCREASE AGENT EFFICIENCY

AI isn't just useful for automating responses to customers. Just as "suggested responses" is more about improving the speed at which the agent can respond, instead of creating a standalone chatbot, AI also has an important role to play in improving the efficiency of agents and managers behind the scenes.

Modern customer care platforms have a role to play interpreting conversations as they come in, in order to better route, prioritize, and analyze the conversations. This includes automatically categorizing the request (is it a baggage issue or a refund issue?). A Visual IVR system can help with a lot of these, but sometimes requests will come in an unstructured text format, or won't fit in the standard IVR options. In these cases, machine learning systems trained on a large data set have an improved accuracy vs. human-coded rules.

An example of this in action is Conversocial's prioritization engine, PRE (Priority Response Engine). Social media (especially public social media) can include a large number of messages that don't require a response. Figuring out exactly how to define whether something is a service issue or not upfront can be difficult using human coded rules. Instead, PRE uses machine learning to train itself based on what agents respond to or not in each account. For example, it would automatically learn over time that the agents from a restaurant chain always respond quickly to anything about wait times, dirt, or food being cold—but that they always ignore when someone posts a check-in to the restaurant location, without any extra comment. If an agent has one hundred conversations to deal with, this brings the ones that need a response to the front of the queue so they are handled first. Conversocial data shows that by doing this, PRE is able to improve first response time by 30–40%, a huge improvement.

CASE STUDY: AUTOMATING BACK-OFFICE BUSINESS PROCESSES WITH WORKFUSION

Workfusion is an AI company based in New York that helps over 250 major organizations to automate their back-office business processing. The cofounders of Workfusion had been working on research at MIT in order to solve two main problems: 1. How to get machines to understand if data were at human quality or not, and 2. How to use machine learning models to automate certain ways of processing this data.

They took the solutions for both of these elements into Workfusion and combined them with robotic components that could manage the input and output of data to and from any system. This enables them to integrate legacy applications that wouldn't otherwise talk to each other—for example, Microsoft Excel with SAP—and to begin to automate tasks, such as invoice processing, that would normally require a human to take data from one system, interpret it, and then output the results into a different system.

A crucial part of their value proposition is that their system can detect when the data it is reading is not at human quality level, and then send these exceptions to the right person to correct and interpret. Over time, the system learns from how humans handle the exceptions, enabling it to automate a greater and greater percentage of processes.

This changes the nature of work for the people who were previously doing the back-office tasks themselves, reserving higher judgment questions for them while the AI handles lower level and repetitive processes.

"It's essential to have the subject-matter experts who understand the correct processes and inputs to train the robots. So instead of typing in the data from an invoice, now they are teaching the system how to read it by highlighting which area relates to a specific input, for example. Their role changes to become robot trainers."

—Adam Devine, SVP and Head of Marketing at Workfusion

Workfusion's system can enable 15–25% efficiency gains on day one using basic, rule based automation, with an extra 20–30% of efficiency coming once their cognitive systems (using Deep Learning algorithms) have been trained by human operators for 8–10 weeks. Over time, the combined system can begin to automate up to 80% of business processes, a huge gain that shows what's possible by combining automation, Deep Learning, and human agents in a single system.

KEY TAKEAWAYS

- The asynchronous nature of messaging enables humans and automation to exist side by side within the same conversation, something that hasn't been possible in any traditional service channel.

- Use Deep Learning based on historical customer service conversations to create a system that can automatically populate responses to common questions. The availability of historical data in the social and messaging environment is a huge advantage compared to other channels.

- Take an iterative approach, starting with suggested responses, then going on to automated responses when the system has a high enough confidence. Gradually automate more as the system continues to learn—but always keep a human agent as a backstop.

- Advanced Deep Learning systems can make use of "short-term memory" to allow them to handle multistep queries.

- Apply AI and machine learning techniques behind the scenes to increase agent efficiency through better prioritization, categorization, and routing.

CHAPTER 10

Adopt a Messaging Approach to all Digital Channels

• •

No company has ever recorded a call for quality purposes.

—Robert Stephens, Co-founder of Assist, Founder of The Geek Squad

By now, the value of messaging as a service channel should be more than clear. But for brands who still have a mix of service channels, there are a number of challenges that remain:

Social volumes spike in crisis situations, requiring the ability to quickly shift agents from other channels

When a crisis comes—which, for many companies, is now a regular occurrence (think every time weather grounds planes)—social explodes. In a typical crisis situation, as discussed in Chapter 6, over 90% of the volume the contact center receives can be over social media. In this situation, companies need to be able to quickly shift agents from other service channels such as chat to focus on the increased social and messaging volumes.

Messaging and chat have the same skill sets, but different workflows mean you can't blend agents

It would be great to be able to seamlessly blend social, messaging, and chat agents. But unfortunately, this isn't as easy as just routing the new social and messaging volumes to your chat agents. Although the skill sets for private messaging are the same, the difference in workflow between web chat and asynchronous messaging make it impossible to blend the agents properly. Instead, agents from chat and other channels will need to switch to a different system and different workflow—only possible if they've been fully trained for these, and even then incurring a delay and downtime while switching platforms.

Different channels and platforms lead to inconsistent customer experiences

Seven out of ten customers rank receiving inconsistent information when contacting brands over multiple channels as a major annoyance[46]—something unfortunately experienced by 65% of consumers.[47] It's a hassle for both the brand and customer if the brand has completely different mechanisms for interacting with customers, and different ways of managing those interactions internally, across channels. It's more work and more expensive in terms of agent handling costs, and it's more complex in terms of managing different systems. Unfortunately, trying to unify customer service delivery is exceptionally hard while there are different teams of agents with different processes and workflows for each channel.

The combined AI + human approach only works with asynchronous messaging

The combination of AI + humans in messaging has the potential to revolutionize customer service by massively decreasing customer effort and improving the customer experience, while simultaneously reducing the cost of service delivery. This is great—but only if all of your customer service queries are over messaging channels.

WHY NOT PUSH ALL YOUR SERVICE VOLUME INTO SOCIAL MESSAGING?

There is one obvious answer to these challenges: *shift all your service volume into social messaging*. If you promote messaging heavily as your primary customer service channel, create a strong brand promise in this channel (that customers will get an in-the-moment response, and be able to fully resolve any issue they have quickly and effortlessly), and turn off access to other digital channels—then you'll be able to execute a major volume shift into messaging, where you can have a single team of blended agents all in the same workflow, a single AI system, and a completely consistent customer experience.

> **What if not all of my customers use social messaging platforms?**
>
> It can be hard to imagine that there are some people out there who aren't on any of the social messaging platforms (although it's hard to get exact metrics, Facebook has almost 100% penetration among the 18–44-year-old age group in the USA), but there are still a small number of people across age groups who remain stubbornly cut off. To ensure complete coverage across every single one of your customers, you can use SMS as a messaging channel that everyone with a mobile phone has, even if it's not a modern smartphone. Although SMS doesn't have the same rich interactive functionality as modern social messaging channels, the workflow is almost identical, and it can combine human agents + AI in the same way.

While I do recommend shifting all of your service volume into social messaging channels, there are valid reasons why some companies aren't yet ready to switch over 100% in this way, for example:

Legal restrictions on sharing customer conversations

For example, medical companies who must remain HIPAA compliant face many restrictions on the kinds of communication they can handle over social messaging versus dedicated, HIPAA-compliant messaging channels.

App businesses (Uber, Lyft, etc.) who have built-in messaging in their platform

Some companies have messaging built into their core applications, or deeply integrated with their core user experience. Depending on the level of integration, it can sometimes still be preferable from a UX and notifications perspective to switch a customer into a messaging application, but there are sometimes reasons to keep the user inside your app.

Using chat to drive website sales

Chat isn't just for service—and many companies, especially in the ecommerce space, use web chat as a carefully managed tool to help drive direct sales. Although it may be possible to replace this use case with socially-enabled messaging platforms in the future, this isn't the case today.

THE ANSWER: TURN ALL DIGITAL CHANNELS INTO MESSAGING

The answer to all of these challenges is to migrate all of your digital service channels into the messaging paradigm. This means ensuring they can:

- Combine real-time and asynchronous messaging
- Have consistent identity across sessions
- Maintain a continuous conversation over time

The good news is that it's possible to deliver this today across web chat and in-app chat as well as social messaging. Switching your chat platforms away from real-time only and into an asynchronous model in this way allows them to sit seamlessly alongside social messaging channels in terms of workflow, agents, and AI.

T-Mobile web chat experience.

T-Mobile mobile chat experience. Requiring customers to be logged in to access chat on both their website and their mobile app allows them to maintain a continuous conversation across both channels—just as if you were switching from desktop to mobile in Facebook Messenger.

With all digital channels designed to work like asynchronous messaging, you can have a single digital agent pool, a single agent desktop, and a single AI system that works seamlessly across all channels.

TURN OFF EMAIL

Social, messaging, and chat are all rated as lower effort channels than email by consumers.[48] In our always on, in-the-moment world, email is often just too slow. The expectation with email is that it needs to be written out more formally, taking longer than just firing off a quick message on your phone; and it could take days to get a response. Email just takes more effort, and will never replace phone calls when a customer has an urgent issue.

Similarly, the much longer form factor of email (instead of a concise back and forth conversation) makes it much harder to use AI to craft a perfect response. AI techniques can still be helpful, but in different ways to how they would be implemented in messaging—requiring a different system and different data set.

Given these challenges, it is better to turn off email altogether—or, at a minimum, stop promoting it as a service channel (keeping it on as a backstop, just as many companies today still receive complaint letters).

DEVELOP FULLY BLENDED AGENTS

Customer service teams have been trying for years to create a fully blended agent model. Unfortunately, this has only really worked in SME or B2B teams, where there are a small number of highly trained agents who are much more focused on customer satisfaction than handling time. The drive for efficiency in larger teams has meant that dedicated teams split by channel type always win out. And nowhere has this pull been stronger than in the social and messaging space, which has often started with completely new teams of agents. But by moving all digital channels into the same messaging paradigm, we will finally enter an age where even large contact centers can employ a blended agent model—with all the benefits that come with this in workforce management (no need to plan exactly how many agents need to be on chat versus email versus social on any one day), training (the same training and processes), and technology (a single agent desktop and platform for every channel).

APPLY THE SAME AI APPROACH (AND DATA) ACROSS ALL CHANNELS

With all digital service channels using the same messaging paradigm, and with the same agent platform, you can start to apply the same AI approach and platform across all of them. This has a huge number of benefits:

1. The same workflow and efficiency gains regardless of where a customer reaches out

2. Historical data and ongoing training can be shared across all channels

Being able to have a single training data set across all channels and having the activity of agents in all channels constantly training and reinforcing the same AI engine will enable the system to learn much faster. This will have an exponential impact on the percentage of queries you are able to automate over time, driving significantly more efficiency gains than if you were only applying Deep Learning on a small subsection of your service volume.

The more data Deep Learning platforms are trained on the more accurate they become.

A SEAMLESS FLOW OF CUSTOMER DATA

The fabled "360° view of the customer" has unfortunately been a pipe dream for most organizations. But with consistent workflow, platforms, and AI systems, unifying customer data across all of your channels starts to become within reach. There are a number of methods to work toward this.

Identity on owned platforms

For messaging on your website or in your app, you have two main options: either apply a "logged-in" approach (like the T-Mobile example) with your own username, or utilize social logins (which Facebook and Twitter make readily available). Even if you don't use social login directly in your web or in-app messaging flow, including it as part of your sign-up or registration flow makes it significantly easier to match users and integrate social messaging with your CRM system.

Twitter login for mobile or website apps.[49]

Facebook login for mobile or website apps.[50]

Identity on social messaging platforms

Within any one social messaging application, customers always have a consistent username[51]—so when the same customer messages you again on Facebook Messenger or Twitter, you always know who they are and can see their full conversation history, regardless of whether they are on web or mobile. However, linking that data back to your customer record (so you can have a single view of the customer across both social and non-social channels) isn't as straightforward. The ideal is to have social login as part of your normal user registration (as above), but failing that agents will need to make the link manually during the customer conversation. This could either be through a specific authentication flow, or it can be by simply asking for their email address or other identifier. Once this connection has been established once it can form a permanent link.

With this connection in place, along with the right technology, a conversation could start on your website, move over to your mobile app, then finish on Twitter—without having to miss a beat, or even change agents.

KEY TAKEAWAYS

- The benefits of the combined AI + human approach in messaging are huge, but limited if a significant part of your service volume is still coming through other digital channels.

- Although the recommended approach is to migrate all your service volume into social messaging, this isn't possible for every company. In this case, the approach instead should be to shift all digital service channels into the messaging paradigm (turning off email, or at a minimum stop promoting it).

- Done successfully, this allows you to have messaging on your website, in your mobile apps, and in social—all with the exact same pool of agents, the same agent desktop, and same AI system across all of them.

- Having the same AI system across all digital channels, with a combined training data set, means you can automate a higher percentage of queries across all channels than if the data were siloed.

- Use social login on your website to create a 360° view of the customer across both owned and social channels, enabling customers to move conversations seamlessly across platforms.

CHAPTER 11

Use Social Agents as the Model for Future Customer Service Teams

● ●

The simplest customer service frustration question of all: "Why isn't this as important to you as it is to me?"

—Seth Godin, bestselling author[52]

Many call centers today are still run like factories, with the seconds counted against every action, toilet breaks monitored, and carefully crafted scripts that state exactly what agents can and cannot say in response to certain queries. But in a world where the majority of simple queries and issues are handled "self-service" by interacting with intelligent agents and bots, and where human agents are only coming in to assist with complex or emotionally charged issues, how does the role of the agent change? As a leader, how should you think differently about how to hire and manage agents in this environment?

In this new world, human agents stop being the front line of customer service, and instead primarily help with escalated issues. With the human cost of delivering service significantly reduced, and AI massively increasing agent efficiency, the cost of resolution, while still important, becomes much less relevant compared to customer experience metrics like CSAT, NPS, and sentiment conversion. Because simple, common queries and tasks will be the easiest to automate, agents will be left to deal with the knotty, complex issues that require them to have more freedom to interact with different parts of the business and get issues resolved, whatever it takes.

This may sound very different to the typical way customer service works today. But the good news is that we already have a model for this exact kind of agent: social care agents.

THE SOCIAL CARE TEAM AS MODEL AGENTS

Social care started as an escalation channel, generally when traditional service channels hadn't worked, and the customer was escalating the issue themselves. Because of the public nature of social and the potential backlash of getting it wrong, many companies put together a team of "ninja agents," often picked out from the "CEO team" (the select customer service team that many companies have to deliver service to the CEO, the CEO's friends and family, and any super-important customers, such as celebrities). These agents are generally more highly qualified than normal, can be trusted (with some training) to respond publicly on behalf of the company, and are able to do whatever it takes across the business to get issues resolved quickly.

As social care has grown and teams have moved beyond just a core group of ninja agents, the core principles have remained. Only the best and brightest of the agent pool join social care teams, with strict requirements around writing skills and personality types. Instead of scripts, they are given a lot of freedom to respond in a human, engaging way (often more informally than typical for the brand). Although measuring their time and efficiency is important, it's second fiddle to doing an incredible job for customers. Many of them are given the freedom to go beyond just solving an issue, and make use of humor in their conversations to great affect.

As the majority of customer service volume shifts into digital messaging, and as more and more of the basic issues are dealt with automatically, the social care team will be a model for the rest of the customer service operation. Managers running social customer care today are the contact center leaders of tomorrow.

In this chapter, I share what we've learned at Conversocial working with hundreds of major organizations around the world as they launch, manage, and grow their social care teams, then look at the broader implications of a reduced agent workforce as automation takes a larger and larger role in the years to come.

THE SIX KEY TRAITS FOR GREAT SOCIAL AGENTS

Great social service agents connect with customers on a personal and emotional level—something that isn't easy over digital, written communication. Building relationships anchored in empathy and connection are critical. There are six key traits that you need every agent to embody, and which you should be checking for as part of your interview process:

Empathy

Do they understand the frustration that customers go through, and have a desire to help? Agents need to be able to put themselves in the customer's shoes, and show real compassion. When a customer is really upset or frustrated, they need to feel that the agent genuinely cares about helping them.

Resilient

Can the agent cope in a crisis situation, and stay calm even with the most upset and unreasonable customer? No matter the context, social agents must be able to react calmly, assess a situation, and respond back to the customer in a personable way. They must be able to show not only patience, but an ability to "role with the punches" by responding professionally in any scenario. Ask interview questions about how the agent has coped with irate customers in the past.

Articulate

Can they communicate complex messages effectively through text in a concise way? Social agents must be able to succinctly and effectively answer potential complex queries in 140 characters. Good spelling and word choice are also important—minor errors can tarnish the brand's appearance and damage credibility with the customer. During interviews, give applicants real questions received over Twitter and ask them to write mock replies.

Curious

Do they have a desire to be constantly improving, learning, and exploring? Whether recruiting internally or externally, it is essential that social customer service agents have the eagerness not only to learn new tools, but also to know the industry. With social and messaging platforms evolving and changing frequently, agents need to stay up-to-date with the latest cultural and social norms. Internal training can help to an extent, but only if the agents are eager to learn.

Confident

Can they trust their instincts to be creative, and are they happy not following a script, even in public? Agents need to be composed and able to act quickly, even if the CEO of your company is being publicly @mentioned in the conversation. On Twitter the world is watching, and agents need to be able to operate under high pressure.

Personable

Can the agent find the right tone of voice, no matter the situation? During the interview process, create a problem-solving scenario that involves the agent having to ask questions about the situation the customer is in. Do they handle this in a friendly, personable way? Does their tone of voice match how your brand wants to portray itself?

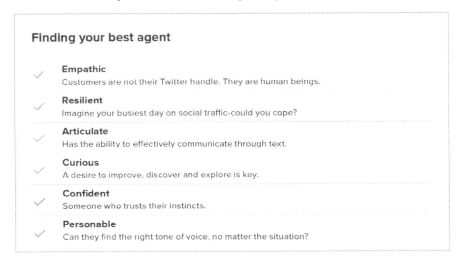

Finding your best agent

✓ **Empathic**
Customers are not their Twitter handle. They are human beings.

✓ **Resilient**
Imagine your busiest day on social traffic-could you cope?

✓ **Articulate**
Has the ability to effectively communicate through text.

✓ **Curious**
A desire to improve, discover and explore is key.

✓ **Confident**
Someone who trusts their instincts.

✓ **Personable**
Can they find the right tone of voice, no matter the situation?

THE IMPORTANCE OF EMPATHY

Some of these traits may sound fluffy. How does this mesh with the push just to make every service interaction as effortless as possible? Well, effortless should be your primarily goal—but if this fails for any reason, and the customer's issue can't be solved quickly or easily (or gets escalated up), then that customer will often be upset and frustrated. In these situations, the ability for the agent to show empathy and to connect is essential.

Studies have found that the emotional satisfaction of a customer after a service interaction can have a major impact on attrition and spend. One major retail bank found that its emotionally satisfied customers had lower attrition and higher spend rates than other customers—even if those customers were rationally satisfied with the resolution[53] (Figures 1 and 2).

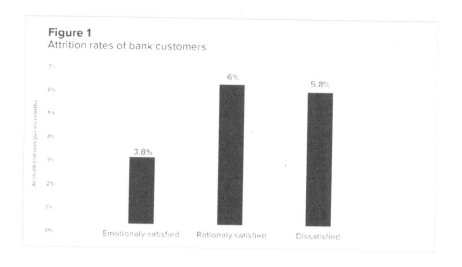

Figure 1
Attrition rates of bank customers

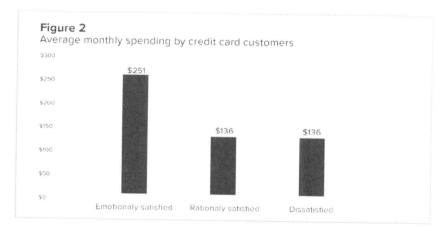

Figure 2
Average monthly spending by credit card customers

Source: Booz & Co[54]

Empathizing with customers is not new, it's just been steamrolled by scripts, cost, and time pressures over the past few decades. Booz & Company (now part of PWC) partner Traci Entel advocated an empathy-based approach to customer service back in 2007 with the publication of the Empathy Engine framework.[55] Entel and her team found that companies that emphasize empathy are able to out-compete and differentiate themselves from the competition because they:

- Understand and resolve customers' problems at minimum cost to customers

- Create a company-wide culture of empathy

- Empathize with and give decision-making power to their frontline employees so they can focus on delivering excellent customer service[56]

As Entel noted in her research, "When a company demonstrates that it can consistently sense and solve its customers' most difficult problems—when it exhibits consistent empathy–it creates unique, sustainable customer relationships that are difficult for its competitors to replicate."[57]

Zappos is one of the leading examples of a customer care culture that gives its agents the time and freedom to be empathetic. Sandi Dolan, a customer service rep at Zappos, remarked how in previous jobs she used to be under time pressure to close a ticket within a set amount of time: "At other jobs I'd be stressed because I'd have to resolve each call in about five minutes in order to make my numbers."[58] It's tough to show empathy when your bosses don't show any.

But at Zappos, they take a different approach, instilling in their agents the values of the company and giving them the freedom to help their customers however they see fit:

> I think the main thing is just trust [the customer service reps] and let them make their own decisions. Most call centers are set up by policies and so the actual person that's answering the phone doesn't really have the ability to do anything. If you... call most customer service places, if you ask for anything that's not normal they have to talk to a supervisor or just say "oh our policy doesn't allow that" and whatever. So we generally try to stay away from policies, we just ask our reps to do whatever they feel is the right thing to do for the customer and the company.

And that's actually really uncomfortable for a lot of reps that come from other call centers. We kind of have to untrain their bad habits. But I think [customer service reps] are generally not happy because they don't have control over the situation whereas at Zappos there's really nothing that a rep can't do so there's no reason to ever escalate.

—Tony Hsieh, Founder of Zappos[59]

The end result? 75% of Zappos purchases are from returning customers, and 44% of their new customers discover them through word of mouth.

SHOULD YOU PROMOTE INTERNALLY OR HIRE EXTERNALLY?

While it can be tempting to think that having a "new breed of agent" requires hiring completely different people, our experience across hundreds of social care organizations is that internal talent is usually the best source. There are a number of reasons for this:

- You'll have a much larger body of work to assess an agent's writing skills and personality—with more limited data, there's always a greater chance of judging an outside hire incorrectly

- The agents will already be familiar with your core contact center operations, allowing you to focus their training on social and messaging

- Since social customer service is a relatively young field, there are very few agents that have "social" on their resume, giving outside recruitment little advantage

In addition to this, social agents are typically seen as the "elite" team within the contact center, and getting promoted into the team can be a very motivating reward for excellent work.

Another common question is whether social agents need to be Gen Y social media natives. Our experience is that with the right training, people of all ages can become expert social agents. Social media knowledge can be taught; the personality traits that make for a great agent are harder to find. But while it's not useful to only try and recruit Gen Y agents for social media, it is useful to try and recruit agents who fit your typical customer profile and demographic. It's easier for agents to empathize with customers and be passionate about the products if they fit the target market as well—and the best customer service agents are genuine brand advocates.

CASE STUDY: USING HUMOR IN CONVERSATION AT WOOLWORTHS

In September 2015, Jamie McGloin made dinner at home and decided to troll Woolworths Facebook Page in Australia, affectionately known as "Woolies" down under. While the water boiled, he seemed unhappy with their spaghetti product and in a fit of creative genius, he hijacked the lyrics from the Eminem song *Lose Yourself*[60] to levy a "spaghetti smackdown" on Woolies.

His post was witty and made for viral gold on social media:

Jamie McGloin ▶ Woolworth's

Yesterday I was searching for food to make my mum's spaghetti. I was nervous, my knees were weak, palms were sweaty and to top it off, I had vomit on my sweater already. To be honest, I was ready to drop bombs, but I kept on spaghetti what I wrote down. I feel I had one shot, one opportunity and I let it slip. I could have seized everything and I left with nothing but a brown onion and tomato paste. I lost myself in the spaghetti because I had spaghetti on my spaghetti already. Snap back to spaghetti. Oh there goes more spaghetti! So today I went back to purchase some spaghetti, instead of finding spaghetti in the packet, I found this. It was spaghetti!!! What should I do with it? Should I return the spaghetti?

Love Jamie xox

Little did he know that Woolworths had an attentive, witty, and culturally attuned social service agent listening who quickly responded in lock step with the original song lyrics:

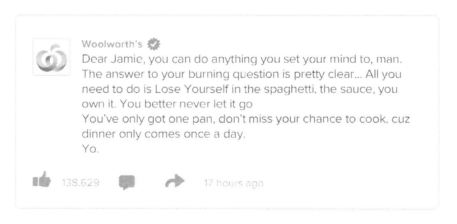

Woolworth's ✓

Dear Jamie, you can do anything you set your mind to, man. The answer to your burning question is pretty clear... All you need to do is Lose Yourself in the spaghetti, the sauce, you own it. You better never let it go
You've only got one pan, don't miss your chance to cook, cuz dinner only comes once a day.
Yo.

And the Woolies social agent didn't stop there:

The Internet loved it:

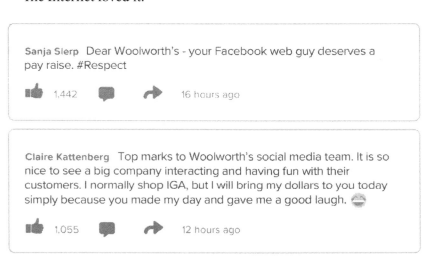

The Woolworths service agent exhibited wit, personality, in-the-moment humor, confidence, curiosity, and empathy—all hallmarks of a great customer service agent for the social messaging era. This was not a scripted, robotic exchange—it was dynamic, authentic, and real. And in return, it got a huge amount of positive viral attention. This is a great showcase of what your customer service agents can do when given the freedom to be creative and human in their responses. As automation starts to handle more and more of the rote replies, agents will be able to focus their energies on providing unique customer experiences such as this one.

A NEW MODEL FOR CONTROL: PEER APPROVAL

Bringing new agents into the social messaging world can be difficult—especially if they are responding publicly, or getting the freedom to be funny and human, for the first time. As a result, many companies have all messages from new agents going through an approval workflow, where more senior managers are checking every response before it goes out. Depending on the level of concern you have around messages, especially public messages, you may want to have approval for every public response going out. But a manager-approval model in this situation will quickly struggle to scale, having a negative impact on response times.

A major, billion-dollar retailer we work with at Conversocial instead utilizes a "peer approval" model. At any one time, one-third of their social agents are in "approval mode," quickly checking over the responses their peers are doing, spotting grammar or spelling mistakes, and giving feedback on humor and tone of voice. This enables them to maintain full approval of all public posts even though they have scaled to hundreds of agents, with over ten percent of all their service queries now coming through social and messaging channels.

Where real-time approval is unnecessary or not possible because of resourcing constraints, it's still essential to have an effective quality assurance (QA) process in place to review responses after the event. This creates a feedback loop, either for managers to discuss the best and worst examples 1:1 with the agent, or in a group setting where you pick out good and bad examples from across the team and brain storm how to improve. It can also be useful to take a look at how other companies are handling their public responses—this is one of the really unique opportunities afforded by the public nature of social care.

Of course, if your agents want to go completely out there with a response like the Woolworths example, the process should be to get this checked by a manager before proceeding.

THE ROLE OF HUMAN AND MACHINE IN YEARS TO COME

A close friend of mine is an industrial entrepreneur with a factory in China. Just two years ago, they had 1,600 employees working in the factory. Then they started to seriously use robotics in the factory. In one year, they had reduced the headcount to 800 people. A year on, and it was just 400 (where he sees it staying for a while). A 75% reduction in workforce in just two years, with the same productivity. Will we see the same changes in the customer service workforce over the next few years?

McKinsey believes that we are in a new automation age (projected to last until 2085[61]), driven by the rise of robotics, AI, and machine learning, with the potential to drive more productivity growth than any era in the past. Unlike the type of automation we witnessed during the Industrial Revolution, during which the steam engine replaced routine physical work activities, the changes we can expect from this new transformative period will center around cognitive capabilities, like consequential decision-making, tacit judgments, and sensing emotion.

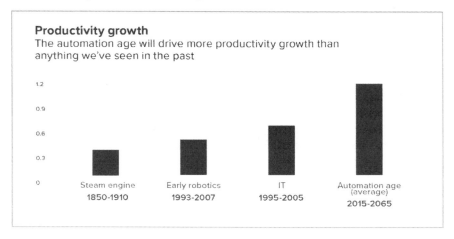

Productivity growth
The automation age will drive more productivity growth than anything we've seen in the past

Source: McKinsey & Company[62]

Instead of predicting the complete replacement of jobs, McKinsey foresees that almost all jobs will be made much more efficient through the automation of certain activities within them. Different types of activities can be automated with different levels of difficulty: whereas predictable physical work (factory workers) and data collection (a customer service rep asking for your flight number) are highly susceptible to automation, stakeholder interactions (dealing with an upset or irate customer who can't fix their issue over self-service) and managing others (the role of a contact center supervisor) are much less susceptible to automation.

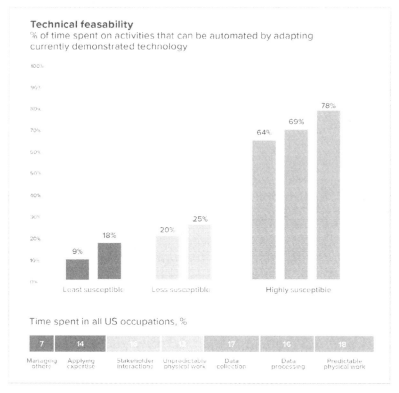

Analyzing work activities rather than occupations is the most accurate way to examine the technical feasibility of automation. Customer service is a mix of "data collection" (easy to automate) and "stakeholder interactions" (harder to automate). Source: McKinsey & Company[63]

The application of the latest AI and automation techniques to customer service, combined with the shift of service volumes into digital messaging channels, will enable huge swathes of rote customer conversations that are currently handled by human agents to be replaced by bots. What will be left will be the kind of human, complex interactions that require common sense, empathy, and the freedom to work outside of any known script in order to fix the issue. These traits—using common sense and emotional awareness to make decisions in new situations—are exactly the ones that machines are worst at. It could be many, many decades before we have AI that is able to make common sense decisions in a completely new environment.

This kind of work, to be done well, requires agents who believe in your brand and are truly knowledgeable about your product. They need to understand your business and how different teams work together. They need to be able to make use of AI and technology to be able to quickly find answers and to minimize errors. And they need to be able to communicate complex issues in simple and concise ways both internally and externally.

These requirements will cause shifts in the job market for customer service (which currently employs 2.7m people in the USA, according to the Bureau of Labor Statistics)[64]. Over the last few decades we saw a huge number of customer service jobs move from Western countries to outsourcers based in lower income and developing countries. But with the shift in requirements caused by the advent of automation, I expect to see a significant shift back toward insourcing—the net effect could even be *more* customer service agents in the US. The Zappos model—where agents are highly integrated, highly motivated full-time employees given a huge amount of freedom to help customers—will become the norm.

Some people are resistant to the changes that automation will bring, especially to the workforce. Even Bill Gates, one of the forefathers of the modern computing era, has called for a "Robot Tax"—arguing that the huge job displacement that will come from automation should be slowed down to give us time to retrain and help people adapt to the new reality.[65] It's true that, as executives today, we need to think about more than just profit, and instead think about all of the stakeholders in our business, including employees. But the drumbeat of innovation will continue to march forward, and the coming together of modern automation and messaging isn't just about saving money (like many of the contact center "innovations" of the past)—it's also about making customer service faster and more convenient for the customer. That factor means that companies that move quickly to embrace the new reality will generate huge competitive advantages in customer loyalty and lifetime value that will make this model the new norm.

KEY TAKEAWAYS

- Whereas contact centers today can operate like tightly controlled factory operations, the contact center of tomorrow—where most simple issues are handled automatically, with only more complex or emotional issues being handled by agents—will instead operate much more like social care teams do today. As such, the social care team is a great model for the customer service team of the future.

- The personality of the social agent is paramount. Can they display empathy, understanding, and humor using the written word, in a concise way? Do they have the confidence to respond publicly on behalf of the brand?

- Although it can be tempting to hire externally, promoting internally will generally get better results, as long as you have the right training in place.

- Empathy is one of the most important traits for social agents, with real business benefits. But agents can only display this if they are freed from scripts and constraints.

- Humor can be a powerful tool to engage with customers, especially in public comments where it can go viral—in a good way.

- Approval workflows can be used to check agent responses, especially when new agents begin to respond publicly. To scale up an approval mechanism, use peer-approval instead of manager-approval.

- An automated future is coming whether we like it or not. Ensure your company and workforce are ready, or you'll be left behind.

CONCLUSION

When I founded Conversocial in 2010, companies were experiencing social crises for the first time, mobile messaging barely existed, and the only places making use of AI were academic research labs, not businesses.

Today, all of these are part of the fabric of our daily lives.

The widespread adoption of smartphones and the development of press-a-button convenience applications that enable us to do almost anything effortlessly have created a growing awareness of the concept of effort among customer service leaders. Over the past few years, I often found myself advocating the concepts behind *Effortless Experience* for the first time to many executives. But today, I'm more likely to find the book already sitting on the desks of most people I visit. As a result, more and more companies are rethinking their service experience through the lens of effort and are taking active steps to measure it throughout the customer journey.

No consumer facing brand today thinks they can ignore social media. Every executive team is on the lookout for any viral event that could blow up into the mainstream press and impact their stock price. And, although there is a wide disparity in how much social messaging care has been operationalized across different businesses, every leading brand has gone beyond basic listening and is at least responding to most queries in social media (even though many are doing so too slowly and some still deflect to traditional channels for resolution).

Artificial intelligence is now all around us. Deep Learning makes your Google search results better. It surfaces the most interesting content in your Facebook feed. It powers Google Translate when you're dealing with colleagues across the pond and across the globe. And Deep Learning ensures your speech is understood when you speak to Siri or Alexa. With many of the leading AI technologies available for free as open source programs, and with cheap and powerful servers that can be spun up in seconds, AI capabilities are now available to any company with a strong engineering team.

The social messaging platforms continue to innovate at a breakneck pace. While I've been writing this book, Apple announced the launch of Business Chat, opening a new messaging channel for businesses through iMessage that will allow consumers to message a business straight from Apple Maps, Safari, and even Siri. Facebook Messenger and Twitter keep improving and iterating on their platforms, releasing functionality to enable bots and human agents to more easily coexist, making it easier to find businesses that provide support, and enabling more ways for businesses to promote private messaging to their customers. Even WhatsApp, which has been unofficially used by businesses for years without any official support, has started to experiment with business accounts—and full API access is expected soon.

The wider technology landscape moves at the same breakneck pace, creating even bigger changes that companies must understand and anticipate. Voice assistants—both on our phones and in our homes—have rapidly become mainstream, and are increasingly connected into both apps and physical devices. Their capabilities as platforms are only just starting to be discovered and fully tested. Artificial intelligence will continue to reach human level accuracy in more and more fields, creating major changes in our lives—from the automation of internal business processes changing how we work, to the automation of our cars which will change the nature of cities and turn commuting into valuable work or leisure time through our connected devices.

More platforms, more channels, and more capabilities—at ever increasing speed.

As an executive in this world that is spinning at the speed of digital, how do you ensure that your customer service function keeps pace? The fact that the majority of customer service issues are still resolved on the telephone—a technology invented in 1876—is a clear indictment of the stark gap between the pace of technological change and the state of customer service.

It's time to close that gap. The tools are available. The know how is available. The computing power is available. It comes down to choosing to embrace change and leading by doing.

Those that lead by early example will no doubt stumble and some will even fall. Yet experimenting, trying and learning is part of doing business in a fast-paced, hyper-connected world. The alternative is not really an alternative at all.

The six pillars for the future of customer care that I set out in Part Two of this book will not only enable you to bring your customer service delivery into the social and messaging era, but will set you on a path to deliver a constantly improving experience to customers as you automate a greater and greater percentage of issues, shift more and more of your service volume into social messaging, and apply the messaging paradigm across all of your service channels.

Often when new consumer technologies and platforms emerge, executives are faced with a choice: do you build a marketing gimmick that will get you some quick headlines or do you figure out how to use the new technology to make your customer's lives easier in a meaningful way? The second may not be so headline grabbing, but it is the hard work that drives real bottom line results. With the launch of the bot platforms, every company has this exact choice: do you build an attention grabbing chatbot that will garner short-lived headlines, but which will not fundamentally change how you serve your customers; or do you build a Visual IVR system using the bot functionality that no one will write about but which has real impact on speed of resolution and the efficiency of your care team? The second is less exciting, and may actually require more education internally to explain, but it's the right choice.

Similarly, gradually applying AI to customer service in the way outlined in this book is a process that will, over time, generate significant results but won't create headlines on day one. Educating internal stake-holders on the value that techniques like Deep Learning will bring over time is hugely important.

For many years, AI has been a dirty word in customer service. During the "AI winter" (the decades where most people had given up on the ability of AI to really have an impact in the real world, or for us to make real progress with concepts like Neural Nets), almost all the "'AI" attempts in customer service were basic, rule-based chatbots that harmed rather than helped the customer experience. And when social media care started, many consumers were using it specifically as a way to find a human connection with brands. They didn't want to speak to a robot—especially if they were using social to escalate an issue from another channel. They had already run into difficulty, and now they wanted a real person to help them get their issue resolved. As a result, the attempts by some brands to build automated bots to respond publicly to care issues over Twitter backfired terribly.

Against this backdrop, our prevailing philosophy at Conversocial was "Humanity at Scale." For many years we avoided most applications of AI. Yes, we used automation in many ways—but always behind the scenes, helping to super-charge human agents and make them as efficient as possible—using intelligent prioritization, advanced routing, automatic content distribution and more. We never used automation to handle actual responses to customers. But the massive advances in both machine learning and bot platforms over the last few years have changed our mindset.

A geek at heart, I've always been fascinated by developments in AI, and it's exciting to now have a chance to implement these techniques in the real world to make a difference with customers. If you're reading this book it's because you are a leader with the foresight to spot the potential that AI has to improve the customer experience, reduce customer effort, and reduce service costs. It is imperative that we stand up in our organizations to educate and spread the word on the benefits that AI can bring, and I hope this book proves a useful tool in aid of this.

To realize the vision of using a combination of messaging, automation, and AI to fundamentally disrupt the customer service model, many elements must come together. Disparate technologies must be integrated in complex ways. Agents need to be retrained with new skills and processes, and possibly even rehired. And consumer behavior has to change so that messaging is their first entry point, even with urgent and complex issues. The six pillars give you a roadmap that could take years to fully implement. But as Lao Tzu said, even a journey of a thousand miles starts with a single step. When you get in the office on Monday morning, there are three immediate steps you can take to get started:

1. Resource social messaging for real-time conversations: For messaging to become a channel that can replace phone calls, customers need to know that if they message you they will get a response in minutes, not hours. Start putting together a resource plan for social messaging that enables this kind of response speed—not just minimum coverage. Make sure you are able to measure metrics like agent utilization and the cost-per-resolution in messaging so that you know how many agents you need, and can make an appropriate investment case.

2. Build your Visual IVR: Make your first foray into automation by planning your first Visual IVR system, using the bot platforms available in messaging to automate the first couple of messages when a customer contacts you. This will help with the routing of issues, improve resolution times, and increase the efficiency of your agents. It's a great first step that can be up and running in weeks and that lays the groundwork for more advanced automation and the application of machine learning.

3. Promote messaging to your customers: With the right resourcing and basic automation in place, you're ready to start really shifting service volume from other channels. Add "Message Us" buttons to your contact pages and websites, and plan a campaign to promote social and messaging care to your customers, both online and offline. You'll be able to quickly increase the volume of private messages you receive, decrease public social complaints, and begin to deflect from other channels.

As you embark on this journey, I would love to hear feedback on what you find works best for you, and what you find challenging. With a continuously evolving landscape, the only way to keep learning is to keep sharing with each other. Message me to continue the conversation!

Joshua March

@JoshuaMarch

NOTES

Chapter 1

[1] YouTube, Mark Zuckerberg's Keynote Address at F8 Conference, April 2016. https://www.youtube.com/watch?v=ouE6qyTc-l0. Accessed July 13, 2017.

[2] Ovum, *"Get It Right: Deliver the Omni-Channel Support Customers Want" (8/16)*. Note: Survey of consumers ages 18–80 in Australia, Europe, New Zealand, and USA.

[3] Matthew Dixon, Nick Toman, Rick DeLisi, The Effortless Experience: Conquering the New Battleground for Customer Loyalty, Penguin Books, 2013, p. 15.

[4] Matthew Dixon, Nick Toman, Rick DeLisi, *The Effortless Experience: Conquering the New Battleground for Customer Loyalty*, Penguin Books, 2013, p. 19.

[5] Matthew Dixon, Nick Toman, Rick DeLisi, The Effortless Experience: Conquering the New Battleground for Customer Loyalty, Penguin Books, 2013, p. 15.

[6] Conversocial Inc., *Social Effort Report: Unlocking Value with Effortless Social Customer Service*, 2017. http://www.conversocial.com/unlocking-value-with-effortless-social-customer-service

[7] Matthew Dixon, Nick Toman, Rick DeLisi, *The Effortless Experience: Conquering the New Battleground for Customer Loyalty*, Penguin Books, 2013, p. 54

[8] IPA Social Works, BT Customer Services: Social Media helped BT improve service and cut costs, https://www.mrs.org.uk/pdf/bt.pdf

[9] IPA Social Works, *BT Customer Services: Social Media helped BT improve service and cut costs*, https://www.mrs.org.uk/pdf/bt.pdf

Chapter 2

[10] Dr. Nicola Millard, BT Global Services, *Serving the Social Customer: How to look good on the social dance floor*, https://business.bt.com/content/dam/bt/business/solutions/3657315/2269710/serving_the_social_customer.pdf

[11] Conversocial Inc., *Humanity @ Scale: How Great Western Railway Uses Messenger for Social Support*www.conversocial.com/case-studies/gwr. Accessed July 13, 2017.

[12] YouTube, *Computer Says No*, https://www.youtube.com/watch?v=A-JQ3TM-p2QI, Accessed July 13, 2017.

[13] American Express, Social Media Raises the Stakes for Service, http://about.americanexpress.com/news/docs/2012x/AMEX_Service_Infographic.pdf, Accessed July 13, 2017.

[14] Ovum, *"Get It Right: Deliver the Omni-Channel Support Customers Want, August 2016*, Note: Survey of consumers ages 18-80 in Australia, Europe, New Zealand, and USA.

[15] Conversocial Report: The State of Social Customer Service. http://www.conversocial.com/hubfs/Conversocial-Report-The-State-of-Social-Customer-Service-16.pdf, Accessed July 13, 2017.

[16] "Consumer Experience Survey" via eMarketer – Feb 2016

[17] Conversocial Inc., *Conversocial Airline Benchmark Report: Going the Extra Mile on the Customer Journey.* http://www.conversocial.com/hubfs/Airline_Report_US.pdf, Accessed July 13, 2017.

[18] Mei Lin Fung, *You Can Learn from "Dell Hell." Dell Did*, Customer Think, March 11, 2008,

http://customerthink.com/you_can_learn_dell_hell_dell_did/. Accessed July 13, 2017.

Chapter 3

[19] Ted Livingston, The Race to Become the WeChat of the West, Medium, November 27, 2014, https://medium.com/@tedlivingston/the-race-to-become-the-wechat-of-the-west-3fe52c8db946#.98h0x6euq. Accessed July 13, 2017.

[20] Telefonica Public Policy & Internet https://www.telefonica.com/en/web/public-policy/-/mensajeria-ott-vs-sms-mensajes-enviados-al-dia-en-millones-

[21] Josh Constine, *How Facebook Messenger Clawed its Way to 1 Billion Users*, TechCrunch, July 20, 2016, https://techcrunch.com/2016/07/20/one-billion-messengers/. Accessed July 13, 2017.

[22] Steven Millward, *WeChat is 5 Years Old. Here's How it's Grow*n, TechInAsia, January 21, 2016. https://www.techinasia.com/5-years-of-wechat, Accessed July 13, 2017.

[23] Business Insider Messaging App Report 2016, http://www.businessinsider.com/the-messaging-app-report-2016-4-23

[24] Shannon Greenwood, Andrew Perrin, Maeve Duggan, *Social Media Update 2016*, Pew Research Center Internet & Technology,

http://www.pewinternet.org/2016/11/11/social-media-update-2016/. Accessed July 13, 2017.

Chapter 4

[25] https://slackhq.com/slack-is-turning-two-477e91f7b277

[26] Elana Zak, *How Twitter's Hashtag Came to Be*, Wall Street Journal, October 3, 2013. https://blogs.wsj.com/digits/2013/10/03/how-twitters-hashtag-came-to-be/ Accessed July 13, 2017.

[27] Chris Messina, January 19, 2016. https://medium.com/chris-messina/2016-will-be-the-year-of-conversational-commerce-1586e85e3991, Accessed July 13, 2017.

[28] Gartner Methodologies, Gartner Hype Cycle, http://www.gartner.com/technology/research/methodologies/hype-cycle.jsp

[29] Connie Chan, *When One App Rules Them All: The Case of WeChat and Mobile in China*, Andreessen Horowitz, August 6, 2016. http://a16z.com/2015/08/06/wechat-china-mobile-first/, Accessed July 13, 2017

[30] Laurie Segall Interview with David Marcus, *FB Messenger Bots Replace Customer Service for Brands*, by Anastasia Anashkina, Susie East, CNNTech. http://money.cnn.com/video/technology/2016/12/06/facebook-messenger-bots-customer-service.cnnmoney/index.html, Accessed July 13, 2017.

Chapter 5

[31] Tanya Dixon, *Microsoft Launches Apache Spark for Azure HDInsight*, GreatResponder.com, June 9, 2016 http://greatresponder.com/page/22/

[32] Cade Metz, *Google's AI Wins Pivotal Second Game in Match with Go Grandmaster*, WIRED, March 10, 2016, https://www.wired.com/2016/03/googles-ai-wins-pivotal-game-two-match-go-grandmaster/?mbid=nl_31016, Accessed July 13, 2017

[33] Laurie Segall Interview with David Marcus, *FB Messenger Bots Replace Customer Service for Brands*, by Anastasia Anashkina, Susie East, CNNTech http://money.cnn.com/video/technology/2016/12/06/facebook-messenger-bots-customer-service.cnnmoney/index.html, Accessed July 13, 2017.

[34] Frank Rosenblatt, *The Perceptron: A Perceiving and recognizing Automation*, Cornell Aeronautical Laboratory, Inc., January 1957, Report # 85-460-1 http://blogs.umass.edu/brain-wars/files/2016/03/rosenblatt-1957.pdf

[35] Yann LeCun List of Publications, http://yann.lecun.com/exdb/publis/index.html

[36] John Markoff, *How Many Computers to Identify a Cat? 16,000.* New York Times, June 25, 2012 http://www.nytimes.com/2012/06/26/technology/in-a-big-network-of-computers-evidence-of-machine-learning.html?pagewanted=all

[37] Kevin Krewell, *What's the Difference Between a CPU and a GPU?* Nvidia Blog, December 16, 2009. https://blogs.nvidia.com/blog/2009/12/16/whats-the-difference-between-a-cpu-and-a-gpu/, Accessed July 13, 2017.

[38] Digital Genius, *KLM Royal Dutch Airlines Case Study.* https://www.digitalgenius.com/casestudy/klm-royal-dutch-airlines-news/, Accessed July 13, 2017.

Chapter 6

[39] Eli Benitez, *Southwest Airlines: Crisis Management in a Live Setting*, October 26, 2016. http://socialmedia.org/blog/southwest-airlines-social-media-case-study-live-from-member-meeting-41/, Accessed July 13, 2017.

[40] Liam Stack, *After Barring Girls for Leggings, United Airlines Defends Decision*, New York Times, March 26, 2016. https://www.nytimes.com/2017/03/26/us/united-airlines-leggings.html?_r=0

Chapter 7

[41] Charles Golvin, *How to Market to Customers via Mobile Messaging*

Gartner, Inc., December 5, 2016 https://www.gartner.com/document/3534818

[42] Charles Golvin, *How to Market to Customers via Mobile Messaging* Gartner, December 5, 2016 https://www.gartner.com/document/3534818

[43] Conversocial, *The Definitive Guide to Social, Mobile Customer Service, 2016.*

[44] Roland Moore-Coyler, *Facebook's AI Tech Mimics How Humans Learn,* The Inquirer, November 16,2015 https://www.theinquirer.net/inquirer/feature/2434242/facebook-s-ai-tech-mimics-how-humans-learn

Chapter 9

[45] Mike Schroepfer, *Teaching Machines to See and Understand: Advances in AI Research,* November 3, 2015 https://code.facebook.com/posts/1478523512478471/teaching-machines-to-see-and-understand-advances-in-ai-research/

[46] http://www.mycustomer.com/community/blogs/pmckean/the-impact-inconsistent-customer-service-has-on-customer-satisfaction

Chapter 10

[47] Peter McKean, *The Impact Inconsistent Customer Service has on Customer Satisfaction,* Mycustomer.com, May 1, 2013. http://www.mycustomer.com/community/blogs/pmckean/the-impact-inconsistent-customer-service-has-on-customer-satisfaction

[48] Aspect Research, 2016, https://www.emarketer.com/Article/Customer-Service-Channels-That-Frustrate-Consumers/1013637, Accessed July 13, 2017.

[49] Twitter Mobile login, https://dev.twitter.com/web/sign-in/mobile-browser

[50] Facebook Mobile login, https://developers.facebook.com/docs/facebook-login/overview/

[51] With some minor exceptions, like someone changing their Twitter handle

Chapter 11

[52] Seth Godin, http://sethgodin.typepad.com/seths_blog/2012/09/the-simplest-service-question-of-all.html

[53] Traci Entel, *The Empathy Engine: Turning Customer Service into a Sustainable Advantage*, Booz & Co., 2007, http://strategyand.pwc.com/media/uploads/The_Empathy_Engine.pdf

[54] Traci Entel, *The Empathy Engine: Turning Customer Service into a Sustainable Advantage*, Booz & Co., 2007, http://strategyand.pwc.com/media/uploads/The_Empathy_Engine.pdf

[55] Traci Entel, *The Empathy Engine: Turning Customer Service into a Sustainable Advantage*, Booz & Co., 2007, http://strategyand.pwc.com/media/uploads/The_Empathy_Engine.pdf

[56] Traci Entel, *The Empathy Engine: Turning Customer Service into a Sustainable Advantage*, Booz & Co., 2007, http://strategyand.pwc.com/media/uploads/The_Empathy_Engine.pdf, p. 5

[57] Traci Entel, The Empathy Engine: Turning Customer Service into a Sustainable Advantage, Booz & Co., 2007, http://strategyand.pwc.com/media/uploads/The_Empathy_Engine.pdf, p. 5

[58] Eric Steuer, *The Jobs Americans Do*, New York Times Magazine, February 26, 2017, p. 43.

[59] https://www.youtube.com/watch?v=c3og1o3nCq0

[60] Mat Whitehead, *This Supermarket Had the Perfect Comeback to a Customer's Eminem Troll*, BuzzFeed, September 29, 2015 https://www.buzzfeed.com/matwhitehead/hope-it-dont-pasta-him?utm_term=.rhv-ZlqP8b#.slDmAgB0G

[61] James Manyika, Michael Chui, Mehdi Miremadi, Jacques Bughin, Katy George, Paul Willmott and Martin Dewhurst, *Harnessing Automation for a Future That Works*, McKinsey Global Institute, January

2017. http://www.mckinsey.com/global-themes/digital-disruption/
harnessing-automation-for-a-future-that-works

[62] James Manyika, Michael Chui, Mehdi Miremadi, Jacques Bughin,
Katy George, Paul Willmott and Martin Dewhurst, *Harnessing
Automation for a Future That Works*, McKinsey Global Institute, January
2017. http://www.mckinsey.com/global-themes/digital-disruption/
harnessing-automation-for-a-future-that-works

[63] James Manyika, Michael Chui, Mehdi Miremadi, Jacques Bughin,
Katy George, Paul Willmott and Martin Dewhurst, *Harnessing
Automation for a Future That Works*, McKinsey Global Institute, January
2017. http://www.mckinsey.com/global-themes/digital-disruption/
harnessing-automation-for-a-future-that-works

[64] Bureau of Labor Statistics, *Occupational Employment and Wages*, May
2016, https://www.bls.gov/oes/current/oes434051.htm

[65] Kevin Delaney, *The Robot that Takes Your Job Should Pay Taxes,
says Bill Gates*, Quartz, February 17, 2017. https://qz.com/911968/
bill-gates-the-robot-that-takes-your-job-should-pay-taxes/